汉英新时代
政经用语精编

A Glossary of Contemporary
Chinese Politics and Economics
Chinese-English

王义端　俞颂熙　编

Compiled by
Wang Yiduan *and* Yu Songxi

FOREIGN LANGUAGES PRESS　BEIJING

目　录
Contents

前　　言

　　中国共产党十一届三中全会以来的二十年,我国又一次经历了历史性的巨大变化。在邓小平理论和党的基本路线指引下,我国改革开放和社会主义现代化建设取得了举世瞩目的辉煌成就。在这一伟大的进程中,我们中华民族的语言也有了新的发展:很多原有的词语获得了新的时代内容,产生了很多的新词语,吸收了一些外来词语。在对外开放不断扩大、对外交流不断发展的条件下,我国新时期的大量用语被迅速翻译成外语。《邓小平文选》,中华人民共和国宪法,以及党和国家的很多重要文献都有了英译本和其他一些外文译本。国务院新闻办公室向全世界发布了一系列的白皮书。中国日报和北京周报等报刊进行了卓有成效的对外宣传报道。这一切十分有利于使世界了解中国,有利于为我国的社会主义现代化建设创造良好的国际环境;同时也为中国人学习外语拓宽了领域,增添了一条重要的渠道。

　　长期以来,我们在学习邓小平理论和重要文献的同时,对照学习《邓小平文选》和重要文献的英译本,收获很大。我们深深感到,这数百万字关于中国改革开放和现代化建设的重要文献的英译本,是凝结着中国翻译工作者集体智慧的文化瑰宝,是他们以创造性劳动奉献给中国人民和世界人民的宝贵精神财富。就翻译创作而言,其中有大量中译英的成功范例,表现出翻译家们的才干和机智,值得每个学习英语的中国人好好研读。在肯定这一主流的同时,我们也看到,在近年的重要文献英译文本中,也出现了某些错译、漏译及翻译偏离原意的情况,存在着缺点和不足。另外,同一中文词语在长时间内有两种或多种译法并存,是相当普遍的现象。对此当然不能一概而论,要作具体分析,但其中确实有一些问题需要研究和认真解决。我们建议,有关部门组织翻译家们首先对一些常用的重要词语如"经济建设"、"精神文明建设"、"民主法制建设"等的译法，进行充分的研讨，统一认识，在翻译上尽可能实现规范化，取得经验后再加以推广。

本书是在长期跟踪学习和对照研读的基础上编写的，以中国改革开放和现代化建设为中心内容，主要从《邓小平文选》与中央重要文献及其英译文本中选择词语，以中英两种语言相对照。选编的词语力求体现邓小平理论的主要内容，体现改革开放和现代化建设的各个方面，体现二十年来在这些方面的英译工作成果，注意避免和纠正译文中曾出现的某些差错，旨在向读者提供一本学习的参考书和实用的工具书。

本书共分为两部分。第一部分是按专题选编的词语。根据江泽民同志在中国共产党第十五次代表大会上的报告的精神列出十四个专题(见目录)，选编了1200多个条目，多数为完整的句子或句子的谓语部分(略去主语，或略去主语和助动词)，也有一部分是词组和短语，按一定的逻辑层次排列。第二部分是按汉语拼音字母顺序排列的用语，大多数为词组或短语，也有一些言简意赅的短句，共有1800多个条目。第二部分的很多用语在第一部分中有实用的例证。

对于同一中文词语的多种不同译法，本书在广泛收集和比较的基础上作出一定的选择。有的只选用一种合理正确并已普遍采用的译法。有的选择或归纳成两种或两种以上各有特色的译法，供选用、参考、借鉴，或供进一步研究之用。

本书可供以下人员使用或参考：有关的英译工作者，需要使用英语的涉外工作者，高等学校英语专业或某些社科类专业的教师、研究生和高年级学生，爱好英语的党政干部。本书对渴望了解中国，正在努力学习汉语并已达到相当水平的外国朋友也有用处。

本书的编写是一个尝试，编者水平有限，欢迎读者多提宝贵意见，尤其要请英语专家和翻译家们批评指正。

编者　1998年12月

用 法 说 明

一、本书第一部分为专题选编。多数专题分若干节,每一节有二级标题。这部分选编的汉语条目有三种类型。一类是完整的句子,后面有句号;一类是句子的谓语部分,略去了主语,或略去了主语和助动词,后面不加句号;还有一类是多字的词组和短语。所有这些条目均按一定的逻辑层次排列。

二、本书第二部分为按汉语拼音字母顺序排列的用语。这部分选编的汉语条目按第一个字的汉语拼音字母顺序排列。同音而声调不同的,按四声顺序排列。第一个字同音同声调的条目,按第二个字的拼音顺序排列。第二个字相同的,按第三个字排列,以此类推。同音同声调而不同形的汉字,采用《现代汉语词典》(修订本)的排列法。

三、在本书第一部分中,一个汉语条目若有两种或两种以上的英译时,分行或分段列出不同译法,每行或每段前冠以(1)、(2)、(3)等符号。序号不表示主次。

如:中国的发展离不开世界。这句话有三种译法,分行列出:

(1) China's development will not ignore the world.

(2) China cannot develop in isolation from the rest of the world.

(3) China's development is inseparable from the world.

在本书第二部分中,一个汉语条目若有两种或两种以上的英译时,用分号(;)将不同的译法分开。如:"经济体制改革"主要有两种译法,其英译条目为 reform of the economic structure; economic restructuring.

四、圆括号( )的用法:

1. 对于同一个汉语条目,若有某些英译路子相同,译法类似,但具体的用词有所不同,则在英译条目中的有关单词或词组后面,使用圆括号,并在括号内使用 or,在

or 后面列出英译中替换使用的词或词组。

如:"流通领域"通常译为 the field of circulation,但近来在有的重要文献的译文中译为 the field of distribution,也不是没有根据,因此在相应的英译条目中就表达为 the field of circulation (or distribution)。

又如:"农产品"的英译有时写为 agricultural products (or farm produce)。

2. 在汉语条目中,有时用圆括号表示括号内的词或词组为或有或无,或可有可无。

如:汉语条目"保险(业)"的相应英译条目为 insurance。这表示"保险"和"保险业"的英译均可为 insurance。

又如:"金融市场(体系)"的英译条目为 financial market (system),这表示"金融市场"的英译为 financial market,同时也表示"金融市场体系"的英译为 financial market system 。

在英译条目中,若圆括号内无 or 或缩略语,则圆括号内的词或词组也是或有或无,或可有可无。

如:"党内监督"的一种英译为 supervision by Party (organizations and) members,意思是有过 supervision by Party members 和 supervision by Party organizations and members 这样两种译法。

3. 有时在汉语条目中使用圆括号,在相应的英译条目中使用圆括号并在括号内使用缩略语 i.e.,以说明某些词组的具体内涵。

如:党际关系四项原则(独立自主,完全平等,互相尊重,互不干涉内部事务)

the four principles for inter-party relations (i.e. independence, complete equality, mutual respect and non-interference in each other's internal affairs)

4. 在汉语条目中,有时利用圆括号列出某些词组的简称或全称。

如:中国人民政治协商会议全国委员会(政协全国委员会);集体经济(集体所有制经济)

5. 在英译条目中,有时利用圆括号列出某些词组的缩略语。

如:"亚太经合组织"的英文名称 Asia-Pacific Economic Cooperation (APEC)

五、方括号[ ]的用法:

使用方括号主要为节省篇幅。方括号内列出的字、词或词组，与方括号前的字、词或词组处于同等地位，可以互相替代。

如：建设有中国特色社会主义的经济［政治，文化］

build a socialist economy［politics, culture］with Chinese characteristics

以上的汉英两类条目实际上各包含三个用语。

词语主要来源

本书主要从以下重要文献及其正式英译文本中选用词语：

《邓小平文选》

中国共产党第十五次全国代表大会文件

中国共产党第十二、十三、十四次全国代表大会文件

中国共产党十一届三中全会以来的中央全会文件（有英译文本者）

中华人民共和国宪法

1992 年至 1998 年历次全国人民代表大会上的政府工作报告

中华人民共和国香港特别行政区基本法

1992 年至 1998 年期间国务院新闻办公室发表的白皮书

党和国家主要领导人的若干重要讲话（有英译文本者）

第一部分
专题选编

PART ONE
Selected Entries
on Special Subjects

一、邓小平理论的历史地位和指导意义
Historical Status and Guiding Significance of Deng Xiaoping Theory

中国共产党以马克思列宁主义、毛泽东思想、邓小平理论作为自己的行动指南。

The Communist Party of China takes Marxism-Leninism, Mao Zedong Thought and Deng Xiaoping Theory as its guide to action.

邓小平理论是马克思列宁主义的基本原理同当代中国实践和时代特征相结合的产物,是毛泽东思想在新的历史条件下的继承和发展。

Deng Xiaoping Theory is a product of the integration of the fundamental tenets of Marxism-Leninism with the practice of present-day China and the features of the times and is a continuation and development of Mao Zedong Thought under the new historical conditions.

邓小平理论是马克思主义在中国发展的新阶段。

Deng Xiaoping Theory represents a new stage of development of Marxism in China.

邓小平理论是当代中国的马克思主义。

Deng Xiaoping Theory is Marxism of present-day China.

邓小平理论是中国共产党和中国人民集体智慧的结晶。

Deng Xiaoping Theory is a crystallization of the collective wisdom of the Communist Party of China and the Chinese people.

邓小平理论坚持解放思想、实事求是,在新的实践基础上开拓马克思主义的新境界。

Deng Xiaoping Theory, adhering to emancipating the mind and seeking truth from facts, explores a new realm for Marxism on the basis of new practice.

实事求是是马克思列宁主义的精髓，是毛泽东思想的精髓，也是邓小平理论的精髓。

Seeking truth from facts is the quintessence of Marxism-Leninism, of Mao Zedong Thought, and of Deng Xiaoping Theory as well.

邓小平理论坚持科学社会主义理论和实践的基本成果，抓住"什么是社会主义、怎样建设社会主义"这个根本问题，深刻地揭示社会主义的本质，把对社会主义的认识提高到新的科学水平。

Deng Xiaoping Theory, upholding the basic achievements of the theory and practice of scientific socialism, has grappled with the fundamental question of "what socialism is and how to build it" and has incisively expounded the essence of socialism, raising our understanding of socialism to a new scientific level.

邓小平理论坚持用马克思主义宽广眼界观察世界，对当今时代特征和总体国际形势进行正确分析，作出了新的科学判断。

Deng Xiaoping Theory, persisting in observing the world in the broad perspective of Marxism, has made new, scientific judgments on the basis of correctly analyzing the features of the times and the overall international situation.

邓小平理论形成了新的建设有中国特色社会主义理论的科学体系。

Deng Xiaoping Theory constitutes a new, scientific system of the theory of building socialism with Chinese characteristics.

邓小平理论为中国共产党认识世界和改造世界提供了新的强大思想武器。

Deng Xiaoping Theory has provided a new, powerful ideological weapon that will enable the Communist Party of China to understand the world and to change it.

邓小平理论是指导中国人民在改革开放中胜利实现社会主义现代化的正确理论。

Deng Xiaoping Theory is a correct theory guiding the Chinese people in successfully accomplishing their socialist modernization in the process of reform and opening to the outside world.

邓小平理论指导中国共产党制定了在社会主义初级阶段的基本路线。

Deng Xiaoping Theory has guided the Communist Party of China in formulating the basic line for the primary stage of socialism.

在当代中国,只有邓小平理论,而没有别的理论能够解决社会主义的前途和命运问题。

In present-day China, it is Deng Xiaoping Theory, and this theory alone, that can settle the issues concerning the future and destiny of socialism.

在当代中国,马克思列宁主义、毛泽东思想、邓小平理论,是一脉相承的统一的科学体系。

In present-day China, Marxism-Leninism, Mao Zedong Thought and Deng Xiaoping Theory constitute a unified scientific system imbued with the same spirit.

坚持邓小平理论,就是真正坚持马克思列宁主义、毛泽东思想。

Adhering to Deng Xiaoping Theory means genuinely adhering to Marxism-Leninism and Mao Zedong Thought.

高举邓小平理论的旗帜,就是真正高举马克思列宁主义、毛泽东思想的旗帜。

Upholding the banner of Deng Xiaoping Theory means genuinely upholding the banner of Marxism-Leninism and Mao Zedong Thought.

在社会主义改革开放和现代化建设的新时期,一定要高举邓小平理论的伟大旗帜,用邓小平理论来指导我们整个事业和各项工作。

During the new period of the socialist reform, opening up and modernization drive, we must hold high the great banner of Deng Xiaoping Theory and apply it to our entire cause and all our undertakings.

用邓小平理论武装全党
arm the whole (or entire) Party with Deng Xiaoping Theory

用邓小平理论教育干部和群众
educate cadres and the masses in Deng Xiaoping Theory

认真学习马克思列宁主义、毛泽东思想、邓小平理论
conscientiously study Marxism-Leninism, Mao Zedong Thought and Deng Xiaoping Theory

学习马克思列宁主义、毛泽东思想,中心内容是学习建设有中国特色社会主义理论。
We should study Marxism-Leninism and Mao Zedong Thought with the focus on studying the theory of building socialism with Chinese characteristics.

深入学习邓小平理论
study Deng Xiaoping Theory in depth

全面、正确领会和掌握邓小平理论的科学体系和精神实质
comprehensively and correctly understand and grasp the scientific system and the essence of Deng Xiaoping Theory

在实践中继续丰富和发展邓小平理论
continue to enrich and develop Deng Xiaoping Theory in practice

二、社会主义初级阶段的基本路线和纲领
The Basic Line and Program for the Primary Stage of Socialism

(一)社会主义初级阶段
The Primary Stage of Socialism

中国现在处于并将长时期处于社会主义初级阶段。

China is currently in the primary stage of socialism and will remain in this stage for a long time to come.

中国必须在社会主义条件下经历一个相当长的初级阶段去实现工业化和经济的社会化、市场化、现代化。

China must go through a rather long primary stage of socialism to accomplish industrialization and the socialization, market orientation and modernization of the economy.

一切从社会主义初级阶段的实际出发。

(1) In everything we do we must proceed from the realities of the primary stage of socialism.

(2) We should proceed in everything we do from the actual situation of the primary stage of socialism.

社会主义初级阶段是逐步摆脱不发达状态,基本实现社会主义现代化的历史阶段。

The primary stage of socialism is a historical stage in which we shall gradually put an end to underdevelopment and realize socialist modernization by and large.

社会主义初级阶段的历史进程,至少需要一百年时间。

It will take at least a century to complete the historical process of the primary stage of socialism.

现阶段我国社会的主要矛盾是人民日益增长的物质文化需要同落后的社会生产之间的矛盾。

The principal contradiction in Chinese society in the present stage is the one between the growing material and cultural needs of the people and the backward production (or the backwardness of production).

阶级斗争还将在一定范围内长期存在，但已经不是主要矛盾。

Class struggle will still exist within a certain scope for a long time to come, but it is no longer the principal contradiction.

在社会主义初级阶段，要把集中力量发展社会生产力摆在首要地位。

During the primary stage of socialism, it is necessary to give first priority to concentrating on the development of the productive forces.

在社会主义初级阶段，要把改革作为推进建设有中国特色社会主义事业各项工作的动力。

In the primary stage of socialism, we should take reform as the motive force for promoting all the work in building socialism with Chinese characteristics.

在社会主义初级阶段，必须正确处理改革、发展同稳定的关系，保持稳定的政治环境和社会秩序。

In the primary stage of socialism, it is imperative to correctly handle the relationship of reform and development with stability and to maintain a stable political environment and public order.

（二）党的基本路线
The Party's Basic Line

全党要毫不动摇地坚持党在社会主义初级阶段的基本路线。

The whole Party must firmly (or unswervingly) adhere to the Party's basic line for the primary stage of socialism.

领导和团结全国各族人民
lead and unite the people of all our nationalities

以经济建设为中心
(1) take economic development as the central task
(2) make economic development the central task
(3) center on (or focus on) economic development

坚持四项基本原则
uphold (or adhere to) the Four Cardinal Principles

坚持改革开放
persevere in (or persist in, or adhere to) reform and opening up (or opening to the outside world)

自力更生
(1) self-reliance
(2) regenerate through one's own efforts

艰苦创业
(1) work hard with a pioneering spirit; work hard and with a pioneering spirit
(2) start undertakings with painstaking efforts

把我国建设成为富强、民主、文明的社会主义现代化国家
(1) turn China into a prosperous, strong, democratic, culturally advanced and modern socialist country
(2) build our country into a socialist and modernized one which is prosperous, strong, democratic and civilized

中国共产党在社会主义初级阶段的基本路线是：领导和团结全国人民，以经济建设为中心，坚持四项基本原则，坚持改革开放，自力更生，艰苦创业，为把我国建设成为富强、民主、文明的社会主义现代化国家而奋斗。

The basic line of the Communist Party of China for the primary stage of socialism is as follows: to lead and unite the people of all our nationalities in a self-reliant, intensive and pioneering effort to turn China into a prosperous, strong, democratic, culturally advanced and modern socialist country by making economic development our central task while adhering to the Four Cardinal Principles and persevering in reform and opening up.

"一个中心、两个基本点",是党的基本路线的简明概括。

"One central task, two basic points" is a succinct summarization of the Party's basic line.

要把以经济建设为中心同坚持四项基本原则、坚持改革开放这两个基本点统一于建设有中国特色社会主义的伟大实践。

We must combine the central task of economic development with the two basic points — adherence to the Four Cardinal Principles and adherence to reform and opening up — in the great practice of building socialism with Chinese characteristics.

基本路线要管一百年,动摇不得。

We should adhere to the basic line for a hundred years, with no vacillation.

(三) 党的基本纲领
The Party's Basic Program

建设有中国特色社会主义的经济,就是在社会主义条件下发展市场经济,不断解放和发展生产力。

Building a socialist economy with Chinese characteristics means developing a market economy under socialism and constantly emancipating and developing the productive forces.

坚持和完善社会主义公有制为主体、多种所有制经济共同发展的基本经济制度

uphold and improve the basic economic system in which the socialist public ownership is dominant and different types of ownership develop side by side

坚持和完善社会主义市场经济体制,使市场在国家宏观调控下对资源配置起基础性作用

uphold and improve the socialist market economic structure so that the market will play a basic role in the allocation of resources under state macro-control

坚持和完善按劳分配为主体的多种分配方式,允许一部分地区一部分人先富起来,带动和帮助后富,逐步走向共同富裕

uphold and improve different modes of distribution with distribution according to work remaining dominant, allowing some areas and some people to become prosperous first so that they can stimulate and help others to become well-off and achieving common prosperity step by step

坚持和完善对外开放,积极参与国际经济合作和竞争

uphold and improve opening up (or opening to the outside world) and take an active part in international economic cooperation and competition

保证国民经济持续快速健康发展,人民共享经济繁荣成果

ensure that the national economy will develop in a sustained, rapid and sound way and that the people will share the fruits of economic prosperity

建设有中国特色社会主义的政治,就是在中国共产党领导下,在人民当家作主的基础上,依法治国,发展社会主义民主政治。

Building socialist politics with Chinese characteristics means managing state affairs according to law (or ruling the country by law) and developing socialist democracy under the leadership of the Communist Party of China and with the people as the masters of the country.

坚持和完善工人阶级领导的、以工农联盟为基础的人民民主专政

uphold and improve the people's democratic dictatorship led by the working class and based on the worker-peasant alliance

坚持和完善人民代表大会制度和共产党领导的多党合作、政治协商制度以及民族区域自治制度

uphold and improve the system of the people's congresses, the system of multi-party cooperation and political consultation under the leadership of the Communist Party and the system of regional autonomy in areas inhabited by ethnic minorities

发展民主,健全法制,建设社会主义法治国家
promote democracy, improve the legal system and build a socialist country ruled by law

实现社会安定,政府廉洁高效,全国各族人民团结和睦,生动活泼的政治局面
create a political situation in which we have social stability, a clean and efficient government and unity, harmony and liveliness among the people of all our nationalities

建设有中国特色社会主义的文化,就是以马克思主义为指导,以培育有理想、有道德、有文化、有纪律的公民为目标,发展面向现代化、面向世界、面向未来的,民族的科学的大众的社会主义文化。
Building a socialist culture with Chinese characteristics means taking Marxism as guidance, aiming at training people so that they have high ideals, moral integrity, a good education and a strong sense of discipline, and developing a national, scientific and popular socialist culture geared to the needs of modernization, of the world and of the future.

坚持用邓小平理论武装全党,教育人民
persist in arming the whole Party with and educating the people in Deng Xiaoping Theory

努力提高全民族的思想道德素质和教育科学文化水平
strive to raise the ideological and ethical standards and the educational, scientific and cultural levels of the whole nation

坚持为人民服务、为社会主义服务的方向和百花齐放、百家争鸣的方针,重在建设,繁荣学术和文艺
adhere to the orientation of serving the people and socialism and the principle of letting a hundred flowers blossom and a hundred schools of thought contend, laying emphasis on progress and boosting academic activities, art and literature

建设立足中国现实、继承历史文化优秀传统、吸取外国文化有益成果的社会主义精神文明

foster socialist culture and ideology by basing ourselves on China's reality, carrying on the fine cultural traditions handed down from history (or the fine historical and cultural traditions) and assimilating the advances of foreign culture

建设有中国特色社会主义的经济、政治、文化的基本目标和基本政策，有机统一，不可分割，构成党在社会主义初级阶段的基本纲领。

The basic targets and basic policies for building a socialist economy, politics and culture with Chinese characteristics are well integrated and inseparable. They constitute the basic program of the Party for the primary stage of socialism.

(四)正确处理社会主义现代化建设中的若干重大关系
Correctly Handling Some Major Relationships in the Socialist Modernization Drive

正确处理改革、发展、稳定三者之间的关系
(1) correctly handle the relationship between reform, development and stability
(2) balance reform, development and stability

正确处理速度和效益的关系
correctly handle the relationship between speed and efficiency (or performance)

正确处理经济建设和人口、资源、环境的关系
correctly handle the relationship between economic development on the one hand and population, resources and environment on the other

正确处理第一、二、三产业的关系
correctly handle the relationship between primary, secondary and tertiary industries

正确处理东部地区和中西部地区的关系

correctly handle the relationship between the eastern part and the central and western parts of the country (or the relationship between the eastern and central-western regions)

正确处理市场机制和宏观调控的关系
correctly handle the relationship between the market mechanism and macroeconomic control (or macro-control)

正确处理公有制经济和其它经济成分的关系
correctly handle the relationship between the public sector of the economy and other economic sectors

正确处理收入分配中国家、企业和个人的关系
correctly handle the relationship between the state, enterprises and individuals in income distribution

正确处理扩大对外开放和坚持自力更生的关系
correctly handle the relationship between opening wider to the outside world and adhering to self-reliance

正确处理中央和地方的关系
correctly handle the relationship between the central (authorities) and the local authorities

正确处理国防建设和经济建设的关系
(1) correctly handle the relationship between national defense construction and economic development (or economic construction)
(2) correctly handle the relationship between national defense building and economic development

正确处理物质文明和精神文明建设的关系
correctly handle the relationship between the promotion of material progress and that of cultural and ideological progress

（五）党的基本方针
The Party's Basic Principle

坚持"抓住机遇、深化改革、扩大开放、促进发展、保持稳定"的基本方针
adhere to the basic principle of "seizing current opportuni-

ties to deepen the reform and open China wider to the outside world, promote development and maintain stability"

三、社会主义的根本任务和
中国社会主义建设的战略步骤
The Fundamental Task of Socialism and
the Strategic Steps for Socialist
Construction in China

(一)社会主义的根本任务
The Fundamental Task of Socialism

社会主义的本质是:解放生产力,发展生产力,消灭剥削,消除两极分化,最终实现共同富裕。

The essence of socialism is liberation and development of the productive forces, elimination of exploitation and polarization, and the ultimate achievement of prosperity for all (or of common prosperity).

社会主义的根本任务是发展社会生产力。

The fundamental task of socialism is to develop the productive forces.

在发展社会生产力的基础上不断改善人民物质文化生活

constantly improve the people's material and cultural life on the basis of development of the productive forces

社会主义要消灭贫穷。贫穷不是社会主义,更不是共产主义。

Socialism means eliminating poverty. Poverty is not socialism, still less communism.

集中力量进行社会主义现代化建设
concentrate on socialist modernization drive

逐步实现工业、农业、国防和科学技术的现代化

(1) realize modernization of industry, agriculture, national defense, and science and technology step by step

(2) modernize the country's industry, agriculture, national defense, and science and technology step by step

必须把经济建设作为全党全国工作的中心,各项工作都要服从和服务于这个中心。

It is imperative to make economic development the central task of the entire Party and the whole country. All our work must be subordinate to and serve this task.

必须把发展生产力摆在首要位置,以经济建设为中心,推动社会全面进步。

We must give top priority to the growth of the productive forces and make economic development our central task so as to promote the all-round progress of society.

发展是硬道理。

Development is the absolute principle.

中国解决所有问题的关键在于依靠自己的发展。

The key to the solution of all China's problems lies in our own development.

抓住时机,发展自己,关键是发展经济。

If we are to seize opportunities to promote our own development, it is crucial to expand (or develop) the economy.

发展生产力要讲究经济效果。

In our efforts to develop the productive forces, we should stress economic results.

一切以是否有利于发展社会主义社会的生产力、有利于增强社会主义国家的综合国力、有利于提高人民的生活水平这"三个有利于"为根本判断标准。

We should judge everything by the fundamental criterion whether it is favorable to (or toward) promoting the growth of the productive forces in a socialist society, increasing the overall strength of the socialist state (or the socialist country) and raising the people's living standards, or the "three favorables" for short.

经济建设必须依靠科技进步和劳动者素质的提高。

In pursuing economic development we must rely on scientific and technological progress and the improvement in the quality of laborers.

(二)分三步走基本实现现代化
Realizing Modernization By and Large in Three Steps

分三步走基本实现现代化的发展战略

(1) the development strategy of realizing modernization by and large in three steps (or in three phases, or in three stages)

(2) the development strategy for the basic realization of modernization in three steps

第一步的目标是解决温饱问题。

The goal for the first step (or The first goal, or The first objective) was to solve the problem of food and clothing.

第二步的目标是在二十世纪末达到小康水平。

The goal for the second step (or The second goal, or The second objective) is to secure a fairly comfortable life for our people by the end of the 20th century.

第三步的目标是在二十一世纪的五十年内达到中等发达国家的水平。

The goal for the third step (or The third goal, or The third objective) is to reach the level of moderately developed countries in the first 50 years of the 21st century.

到二○○○年在人口增长 3 亿的情况下，我们将实现人均国民生产总值比一九八○年翻两番。

By the year 2000 we expect to quadruple our 1980 per capita GNP* despite a net population increase of 300 million.

二十一世纪第一个十年将实现国民生产总值比

---

* GNP = gross national product

二〇〇〇年翻一番,使人民的小康生活更加宽裕,形成比较完善的社会主义市场经济体制。

In the first decade of the 21st century, the GNP will double that of the year 2000, the people will enjoy an even more comfortable life and a more or less ideal socialist market economy will have come into being.

再经过十年的努力,到建党一百周年时,使国民经济更加发展,各项制度更加完善。

With the efforts to be made in another decade when the Party celebrates its centenary, the national economy will be more developed and the various systems will be further improved.

到二十一世纪中叶建国一百周年时,基本实现现代化,建成富强民主文明的社会主义国家。

By the middle of the 21st century when the People's Republic celebrates its centenary, the modernization program will have been accomplished by and large and China will have become a prosperous, strong, democratic and culturally advanced socialist country.

在现代化建设的长过程中要抓住时机,争取出现若干个发展速度比较快、效益又比较好的阶段,每隔几年上一个台阶。

In the prolonged process of modernization we should seize all opportunities to bring about several periods of rapid growth with good economic returns, reaching a new stage every few years.

我们要积极推进经济体制和经济增长方式的根本转变,努力实现"九五"计划和二〇一〇年远景目标,为二十一世纪中叶基本实现现代化打下坚实基础。

We must vigorously promote the fundamental shift of economic system and of the mode of economic growth, fulfill the Ninth Five-Year Plan and attain the Long-Range Objectives Through the Year 2010 so as to lay a solid foundation for achieving basic modernization by the middle of the 21st century.

从计划经济体制向社会主义市场经济体制的转变

the shift from a planned economy to a socialist market economy

经济增长方式从粗放型向集约型的转变

（1）the shift from extensive mode to intensive mode in economic growth

（2）the shift from an extensive economic growth mode to an intensive economic growth mode

四、改革开放
Reform and Opening Up

新时期最鲜明的特点是改革开放。

The dominant feature of the new period is the policy of reform and opening to the outside world (or reform and opening up).

改革开放是中国实现社会主义现代化的必由之路。

Reform and opening up are the only way to realize China's socialist modernization.

坚持改革开放是决定中国命运的一招。

The future of China hinges on our adhering to reform and opening up.

在整个改革开放的过程中，必须始终坚持四项基本原则。

Throughout the process of reform and opening up, we must adhere to the Four Cardinal Principles.

必须把改革开放同四项基本原则统一起来。

We must integrate the reform and opening up with the Four Cardinal Principles.

（一）改革——中国的第二次革命
Reform: China's Second Revolution

我们所有的改革都是为了一个目的，就是扫除发展社会生产力的障碍。

All our reforms have the same aim: to clear away the obstacles to the development of the productive forces.

革命是解放生产力，改革也是解放生产力。

Revolution means the emancipation (or liberation) of the productive forces, and so does reform.

改革是中国解放和发展生产力的必由之路。
Reform is the only way for China to liberate and develop its productive forces.

改革是中国的第二次革命。
Reform is China's second revolution.

改革是社会主义制度的自我完善和发展。
(1) Reform is a self-improvement and self-development of the socialist system.
(2) Reform is part of the self-perfecting and self-developing process of the socialist system.

改革是发展的动力。
Reform is the motive force for development.

改革是推进建设有中国特色社会主义事业各项工作的动力。
Reform is the motive force for promoting all the work in building socialism with Chinese characteristics.

我们的改革是全面的改革。
Ours is a comprehensive reform.

我们的改革不能离开社会主义道路,不能没有共产党的领导。
Our reform cannot depart from socialism and it cannot be accomplished without the leadership of the Communist Party.

经济体制改革
(1) reform of the economic structure
(2) economic restructuring

农村改革
rural reform

城市改革
urban reform

国有企业改革

the reform of state-owned enterprises

政治体制改革
（1）reform of the political structure
（2）political restructuring

党和国家领导制度的改革
reform of the system of Party and state leadership

行政体制改革
reform of the administrative system

科技体制改革
（1）reform of the science and technology management
system
（2）reform of the system for managing science and technology
（3）reform of the management system of science and
technology

教育体制改革
（1）reform of the educational structure
（2）reform of the management system of education

高等教育管理体制改革
reform of the management system of higher education

文化体制改革
reform of the system for managing cultural undertakings

人事制度改革
reform of the personnel system

干部制度改革
reform of the cadre system

开放也是改革。
（1）Opening up is also a part of reform.
（2）Pursuing an open policy also means carrying out reform.

（二）对外开放
Opening to the Outside World

现在的世界是开放的世界。
The current world is an open one.

中国的发展离不开世界。
(1) China's development will not ignore the world.
(2) China cannot develop in isolation from the rest of the world.
(3) China's development is inseparable from the world.

对外开放是中国实现社会主义现代化的必要条件。
Opening to the outside world is an essential condition for China to achieve its socialist modernization.

独立自主不是闭关自守，自力更生不是盲目排外。
Independence does not mean shutting the door on the world, nor does self-reliance mean blind opposition to everything foreign.

必须在自力更生的基础上实行对外开放。
It is imperative to pursue the policy of opening to the outside world on the basis of persisting in self-reliance.

对外开放是一项长期的基本国策。
Opening to the outside world is a long-term basic state policy.

广泛吸收和借鉴世界各国包括资本主义发达国家创造的一切先进文明成果
extensively absorb and use for reference (or draw on) all results of advanced civilization created by all other countries including developed capitalist countries

积极参与国际经济技术合作和竞争
take an active part in international economic and technological cooperation and competition

发展对外经济技术交流和合作

develop economic and technological exchanges and cooperation with foreign countries

利用外资
use (or utilize) foreign capital (or foreign funds)

引进国外先进技术和管理经验
introduce (or import) from abroad the advanced technology and managerial expertise (or management expertise)

利用国内国外两个市场、两种资源
make use of both domestic and foreign markets and resources

积极发展对外贸易
actively develop foreign trade

发展开放型经济
develop an open economy

发展外向型经济
develop an export-oriented economy

全方位、多层次、宽领域的对外开放格局
(1) a pattern of opening up in all directions, at all levels and in a wide range
(2) an all-directional, multi-layer and wide-range pattern of opening up
(3) an omni-directional, multi-level and wide-range opening to the outside world

经济特区
special economic zone

沿海开放城市
open coastal cities

沿海经济开放区
open coastal economic development area

经济技术开发区
economic and technological development zone

上海浦东新区的开发开放

the development and opening of the Pudong New Area in (or of) Shanghai

以上海浦东开发开放为龙头，进一步开放长江沿岸城市

open more cities along the Yangtze River, while concentrating on the development and opening of the Pudong Area of Shanghai

开放沿边地区

open the areas along the borders

开放沿交通干线地区

open the areas along main communications lines

开放内陆中心城市

open the major cities in the hinterland

经济领域的开放

opening-up in economic field (or sphere, or domain)

科技、教育、文化等领域的开放

opening-up in scientific, technological, educational, cultural and other fields (or spheres, or domains)

向所有国家开放

be open to all other countries

正确处理对外开放同独立自主、自力更生的关系，维护国家经济安全。

We must correctly handle the relationship of opening up versus independence and self-reliance, and safeguard the economic security of the country.

五、经济体制改革
Economic Restructuring

（一）建立社会主义市场经济体制
Establishing a Socialist Market Economy

计划多一点还是市场多一点，不是社会主义与资本主义的本质区别。

The proportion of planning to market forces is not the essential difference between socialism and capitalism.

计划经济不等于社会主义，资本主义也有计划；市场经济不等于资本主义，社会主义也有市场。计划和市场都是经济手段。

A planned economy is not equivalent to socialism, because there is planning under capitalism too; a market economy is not equivalent to capitalism, because there are markets under socialism too. Planning and market forces (or market regulation) are both means of controlling economic activity.

我国经济体制改革的目标是建立社会主义市场经济体制。

The objective of the reform of China's economic structure is to establish a socialist market economy.

把社会主义同市场经济结合起来，是一个伟大创举。

It is a great pioneering undertaking to combine socialism with the market economy.

积极推进从计划经济体制向社会主义市场经济体制的转变

vigorously promote the shift from a planned economy to a socialist market economy

要坚持社会主义市场经济的改革方向，使改革在一些重大方面取得新的突破。

Keeping to the orientation of the reform for building a socialist market economy, we must strive for new breakthroughs in some major aspects of our reform.

(二) 调整和完善所有制结构
Readjusting and Improving the Ownership Structure

社会主义市场经济是同社会主义基本制度结合在一起的。

The socialist market economy is integrated with the basic system of socialism.

我国是社会主义国家,必须坚持公有制作为社会主义经济制度的基础。

Being a socialist country, China must keep to public ownership as the foundation of its socialist economic system.

我国处在社会主义初级阶段,需要在公有制为主体的条件下发展多种所有制经济。

Being in the primary stage of socialism, China needs to develop diverse forms of ownership (or to develop different types of ownership) with public ownership in the dominant position.

一切符合"三个有利于"的所有制形式都可以而且应该用来为社会主义服务。

Any form of ownership that meets the criterion of the "three favorables" can and should be utilized to serve socialism.

公有制为主体、多种所有制经济共同发展,是我国社会主义初级阶段的一项基本经济制度。

It is a basic economic system for the primary stage of socialism in China to retain a dominant position for public ownership and to develop diverse forms (or different types) of ownership side by side.

坚持以公有制为主体、多种经济成分共同发展的方针

（1）uphold the principle of keeping public ownership in a dominant position and developing diversified economic sectors side by side

（2）uphold the principle of taking the public ownership as the mainstay and allowing diverse sectors of the economy to develop side by side

调整和完善所有制结构
readjust and improve the ownership structure

公有制经济包括国有经济和集体经济,还包括混合所有制经济中的国有成分和集体成分。

The public sector of the economy includes the state-owned and collectively owned sectors, and the state-owned and collectively owned elements in the sector of the economy with（or under）mixed ownership as well.

公有制的主体地位主要体现在:公有资产在社会总资产中占优势;国有经济控制国民经济命脉,对经济发展起主导作用。

The dominant position of public ownership should manifest itself mainly as follows: Public assets dominate in the total assets in society and the state-owned sector controls the lifeblood of the national economy and plays a leading role in economic development.

公有资产占优势,要有量的优势,更要注重质的提高。

Dominance of the public assets should feature in quantitative terms, but more so in terms of improved quality.

国有经济是国民经济中的主导力量。

The state-owned economy（or state-owned sector of the economy）is the leading force in the national economy.

国有经济起主导作用,主要体现在控制力上。

The leading role of the state-owned economy should manifest itself mainly in its control power.

要从战略上调整国有经济布局。

We should make a strategic readjustment in the distribution of the state-owned economy.

对关系国民经济命脉的重要行业和关键领域,国有经济必须占支配地位。

The state-owned sector must be in a dominant position in major industries and key areas that concern the life-blood of the national economy.

提高国有资产在各个领域的整体质量

improve the quality of the state assets as a whole in various areas

增强国有经济的控制力和竞争力

strengthen the control power and competitive power of the state-owned economy

集体所有制经济是公有制经济的重要组成部分。

The collectively owned sector (of the economy) is an important component of the public sector of the economy.

要支持、鼓励和帮助城乡多种形式集体经济的发展。

We should support, encourage and help all forms of collective economy in their development in the urban and rural areas.

公有制实现形式可以而且应当多样化。

(1) The forms for materializing (or realizing) the public ownership can and should be diversified.

(2) Public ownership can and should take diversified forms.

一切反映社会化生产规律的经营方式和组织形式都可以大胆利用。

All management methods (or operation methods) and organizational forms that mirror (or reflect) the laws governing socialized production may be utilized boldly.

要努力寻找能够极大促进生产力发展的公有制实现形式。

We should strive to seek various forms for materializing public ownership that can greatly promote the growth of the productive forces.

股份制是现代企业的一种资本组织形式,资本主义可以用,社会主义也可以用。

The joint stock system (or shareholding system) is a form of capital organization of modern enterprises. It can be used both under capitalism and under socialism.

不能笼统地说股份制是公有还是私有,关键看控股权掌握在谁手中。

We cannot say in general terms that the joint stock system is public or private, for the key lies in who holds the controlling share.

国家和集体控股,具有明显的公有性,有利于扩大公有资本的支配范围,增强公有制的主体作用。

If the state or a collective holds the controlling share, it obviously shows the characteristics of public ownership, which is favorable to expanding the area of control by public capital and enhancing the dominant role of public ownership.

要支持和引导多种多样的股份合作制经济,使之逐步完善。

We should support and guide diverse forms of joint stock partnership and improve them step by step.

非公有制经济是我国社会主义市场经济的重要组成部分。

The non-public sector is an important component part of China's socialist market economy.

对个体、私营等非公有制经济要继续鼓励、引导,使之健康发展。

We should continue to encourage and guide the non-public sector of the economy comprising self-employed and private businesses to facilitate its sound development.

健全财产法律制度
improve the legal system concerning property

依法保护各类企业的合法权益和公平竞争

protect the legitimate rights and interests of and fair competition among all types of enterprises according to law

依法对各类企业进行监督管理

exercise supervision and control over all types of enterprises according to law

（三）加快推进国有企业改革
Accelerating the Reform of State-owned Enterprises

国有企业是我国国民经济的支柱。

State-owned enterprises constitute the pillar of China's national economy.

把国有企业改革作为经济体制改革的中心环节

take the reform of state-owned enterprises as the central link (or key link, or pivotal point) in economic restructuring

要走出一条具有中国特色的国有企业改革和发展的路子。

(1) We must blaze a path with Chinese characteristics for the reform and development of state-owned enterprises.

(2) We have to find a way with Chinese characteristics to reform and develop state-owned enterprises.

建立现代企业制度是国有企业改革的方向。

The establishment of a modern enterprise system is the orientation of the reform of state-owned enterprises.

现代企业制度的基本特征是"产权清晰、权责明确、政企分开、管理科学"。

The basic features of a modern enterprise system are: "clearly established ownership, well defined power and responsibility, separation of enterprise from administration, and scientific management".

以公有制为主体的现代企业制度是社会主义市场经济体制的基础。

A modern enterprise system with public ownership as its mainstay is the foundation of a socialist market economy.

要按照建立现代企业制度的要求,对国有大中型企业实行规范的公司制改革,使企业成为适应市场的法人实体和竞争主体。

We shall carry out a reform to convert large and medium-sized state-owned enterprises into standard corporations according to the requirements of establishing a modern enterprise system so that they will become corporate entities and competitors adaptable to the market.

国家按投入企业的资本额享有所有者权益,对企业的债务承担有限责任;企业依法自主经营,自负盈亏。

The state will enjoy the owner's equity according to the amount of capital it has put into the enterprises and bear limited responsibilities for the debts of enterprises while enterprises will operate independently according to law, responsible for their own profits and losses.

采取多种方式,包括直接融资,充实企业资本金

adopt all kinds of possible means, including direct financing, to replenish the capital funds of enterprises

培育和发展多元化投资主体

cultivate and develop a diversity of investors

推动政企分开

push the separation of the functions of the government from those of enterprises

以建立现代企业制度为方向,切实转换企业经营机制

change in real earnest the way enterprises operate, with the establishment of a modern enterprise system as the orientation

把国有企业改革同改组、改造、加强管理结合起来。

(1) We should combine the reform of state-owned enterprises with their reorganization, upgrading and better management.

(2) We should combine the reform of state-owned enterprises with their reorganization, transformation and strengthening of management.

(3) We should combine our efforts to reform state-owned enterprises with efforts to reorganize, upgrade and exercise more effective management of them.

要着眼于搞好整个国有经济,抓好大的,放活小的,对国有企业实施战略性改组。

Aiming at improving the state sector of the economy (or the state-owned economy) as a whole, we shall effectuate (or carry out) a strategic reorganization of state-owned enterprises by well managing large enterprises (or managing large enterprises well) while adopting a flexible policy toward small ones.

推动国有存量资产的流动和重组
give impetus to the flow and reorganization of state-owned inventory assets

以资本为纽带,通过市场形成具有较强竞争力的跨地区、跨行业、跨所有制和跨国经营的大企业集团。

By using capital as the bonds and relying on the market forces, we shall establish highly competitive large enterprise groups with cross-regional, inter-trade, cross-ownership and transnational operations.

采取改组、联合、兼并、租赁、承包经营和股份合作制、出售等形式,加快放开搞活国有小型企业的步伐。

We shall quicken the pace in adopting a flexible policy toward small state-owned enterprises and invigorating them by way of reorganization, association, merger, leasing, contract operation, joint stock partnership or sell-off.

推进企业技术进步
promote technological progress of enterprises

鼓励、引导企业和社会的资金投向技术改造
encourage and channel the flow of funds of enterprises and society into technological upgrading (or technological transformation, or technical transformation)

形成面向市场的新产品开发和技术创新机制
form a new mechanism for the development of market-

oriented new products and technological (or technical) innovations

加强科学管理
strengthen scientific management

探索符合市场经济规律和我国国情的企业领导体制和组织管理制度
try to institute in enterprises a system of leadership and a system of organization and management that conform to the law of the market economy and the national conditions

建立决策、执行和监督体系
set up a decision-making, enforcement and supervision system

形成有效的激励和制约机制
form an effective incentive and control mechanism

建设好企业领导班子
(1) improve the leadership of enterprises
(2) improve the leading bodies of enterprises
(3) build sound leading bodies of enterprises

发挥企业党组织的政治核心作用
give play to the role of Party organizations in enterprises as political nuclei

坚持全心全意依靠工人阶级的方针
adhere to the principle of relying on the working class wholeheartedly

加强企业经营管理者队伍的建设
(1) strengthen (the building of) the contingent of enterprise managers
(2) improve the contingent of enterprise managers

完善对经营者的选聘、监督、考核和奖惩办法
improve the methods of selecting, supervising, examining, rewarding and punishing managers

加强企业经营管理

improve the operation and management of enterprises

提高企业的整体素质
improve the overall quality of enterprises

鼓励兼并,规范破产,下岗分流,减员增效和实施再就业工程
encourage merger of enterprises (or encourage mergers), standardize bankruptcy procedures, divert (or redirect) laid-off workers, increase efficiency by downsizing (or by reducing) staff and implement re-employment projects (or re-employment programs)

形成优胜劣汰的竞争机制
form a competitive mechanism for selecting the superior and eliminating the inferior

保障下岗职工的基本生活
guarantee the basic needs of laid-off workers

作好下岗职工的再就业工作
(1) assist laid-off workers to find new jobs
(2) make a good job of re-employment of laid-off workers

搞好职业培训,拓宽就业门路,推进再就业工程
(1) organize job training, open up new avenues of employment and promote the re-employment projects
(2) do well in vocational training and create more job opportunities so as to promote re-employment projects

建立全方位、多渠道、多领域的再就业体系
establish a system of re-employment in all directions, through many channels and in many domains

积极推进各项配套改革
press ahead with all the supportive reforms

建立有效的国有资产管理、监督和营运机制
build an effective mechanism for the management, supervision and operation of state assets

保证国有资产的保值增值
guarantee to preserve and increase the value of state assets

防止国有资产流失
prevent the loss of state assets

建立社会保障体系，提供最基本的社会保障
build a social security system to provide the most basic social security

加快职工基本养老保险、医疗保险、失业保险等社会保障制度的改革
accelerate (or quicken) the reform of the social security system including workers' basic old-age insurance, medical insurance and unemployment insurance

加快住房制度改革
accelerate the reform of the housing system

努力开创国有企业改革和发展的新局面
strive to create a new situation (or to break fresh ground) in the reform and development of state-owned enterprises

（四）完善分配结构和分配方式
Improving the Structure and Mode of Distribution

坚持按劳分配为主体、多种分配方式并存的制度
keep to the system in which distribution according to work is primary and a variety of modes of distribution coexist (or diverse distribution modes coexist)

把按劳分配和按生产要素分配结合起来
combine remuneration according to work and remuneration according to (essential) factors of production put in

效率优先，兼顾公平
give priority to efficiency with due consideration to equity

依法保护合法收入
protect lawful incomes according to law

允许和鼓励一部分人通过诚实劳动和合法经营先富起来

allow and encourage some (of the) people to become prosperous (or to get wealthy, or to grow rich) first through honest labor and lawful operations

允许和鼓励资本、技术等生产要素参与收益分配

allow and encourage the use of capital, technology and other factors of production to participate in the distribution of gains

取缔非法收入
(1) ban illegal earnings
(2) ban unlawful incomes
(3) outlaw illicit incomes

整顿不合理收入
(1) take stock of irrational incomes
(2) check (or rectify) irrational incomes

调节过高收入
regulate the excessively high incomes

完善个人所得税制,开征遗产税等新税种
improve the individual income tax system, and introduce such new taxes as inheritance tax

规范收入分配,使收入差距趋向合理,防止两极分化
standardize income distribution so as to make income gaps more reasonable and prevent polarization

要正确处理国家、企业、个人之间和中央与地方之间的分配关系。
It is necessary to correctly handle the relations of distribution among (or between) the state, enterprises and individuals and between the central and local authorities.

逐步提高财政收入占国民生产总值的比重和中央财政收入占全国财政收入的比重
gradually raise the proportion of fiscal revenue in the gross national product and the proportion of the central govern-

ment revenue in the national revenue

调整财政收支结构,建立稳固、平衡的国家财政
adjust the revenue and expenditure structure and establish secure and balanced state finances

(五)市场机制与宏观调控
Market Mechanism and Macroeconomic Control

要加快国民经济市场化的进程。
We should accelerate the process of building a complete market system in the national economy.

充分发挥市场机制作用
give full play to the role of the market mechanism

发挥市场对资源配置的基础性作用
give play to the basic role of the market in the allocation of resources

使经济活动遵循价值规律的要求,适应供求关系的变化
subject economic activity to the law of value and make it responsive to the changing relations between supply and demand

形成有利于市场公平竞争和资源优化配置的经济运行机制
(1) work out a way of operating the economy that favors fair competition in the market and optimal allocation of resources
(2) form an economic operating mechanism that is conducive to fair competition in the market and optimal allocation of resources

发展各类市场,着重发展资本、劳动力、技术等生产要素市场
develop all kinds of markets, with emphasis on markets for capital, labor, technology and other production factors (or other factors of production, or other essential factors of produc-

tion)

商品市场
commodity market

生产资料市场
(1) capital goods market
(2) market for means of production

消费品市场
consumer goods market

金融市场
financial market

资本市场
capital market

证券市场
securities market

劳动力市场
labor market

技术市场
technology market

信息市场
information market

房地产市场
real estate market

市场竞争主体
(1) market competitor
(2) principal in market competition

市场中介组织
intermediary market organization

建立以市场形成价格为主的价格机制
establish a mechanism for pricing mainly by market forces

完善生产要素价格形成机制

improve the mechanism for pricing production factors

改革流通体制
reform the circulation system（or the distribution system）

健全市场规则
improve market rules

加强市场管理
strengthen market management

清除市场障碍
remove obstacles to market development

打破地区封锁和部门垄断
break（through）regional blockades and sectoral monopolies

建成统一开放、竞争有序的市场体系
build up a unified and open market system with orderly competition

加强和改善国家对经济的宏观调控
（1）strengthen and improve the state's macro-control over the economy
（2）strengthen and improve macro-control of the economy by the state

健全宏观调控体系
improve the macroeconomic control system（or the macro-control system）

实现市场机制和宏观调控的有机结合
integrate the market mechanism with macro-control organically

保持经济总量平衡
（1）keep a balance between total demand and total supply
（2）maintain a balance in total supply and demand
（3）keep the overall economic balance

抑制通货膨胀
（1）curtail（or curb）inflation

(2) control inflation

(3) keep inflation under control

促进重大经济结构优化

promote the optimization of the major economic structures

实现经济稳定增长

achieve stable economic growth

宏观调控主要运用经济手段和法律手段。

In macroeconomic control, we should mainly employ economic and legal means.

完善宏观调控手段和协调机制

improve the means of macroeconomic control and the co-ordinating mechanism

金融是现代经济的核心。

Finance is the core of the modern economy.

深化金融体制改革

deepen the reform of the banking system (or the financial system)

建立与社会主义市场经济发展相适应的金融机构体系、金融市场体系和金融调控监管体系

establish a system of financial institutions, a financial market system and a financial supervision and control system which conform to the development of socialist market economy

依法加强对金融机构和金融市场包括证券市场的监管

in accordance with the law, strengthen the supervision and control of the financial institutions and markets, including the securities market

完善和强化中国人民银行的金融调控和监管

improve and strengthen the financial control and supervision by the People's Bank of China

健全金融法规

improve financial statutes

规范和维护金融秩序
standardize and safeguard the financial order

提高金融业经营和管理水平
（1）raise the operational and managerial level in finance
（2）improve the operation and management in finance

有效防范和化解金融风险
（1）effectively guard against and eliminate financial risks
（2）take effective measures to prevent and eliminate financial risks

维护国家金融安全
safeguard the financial security of the country

深化财政体制[财税体制]改革
deepen the reform of the fiscal system [fiscal and taxation systems]

实施适度从紧的财政政策和货币政策
carry out appropriately tight（or stringent）financial and monetary policies

深化计划体制改革
deepen the reform of the planning system

国家计划要体现发展社会主义市场经济的要求。
The state plan must reflect the requirements of developing a socialist market economy.

国家计划要突出宏观性、战略性和政策性。
It is imperative to emphasize the macro-economic, strategic and policy-related characteristics of the state plan.

稳中求进
seek progress amid stability

保持高增长、低通胀的良好发展势头
maintain the good momentum of development featuring high economic growth and low inflation（or featuring a high economic growth rate with low inflation）

六、经济发展战略
Economic Development Strategy

保持国民经济持续快速健康发展

maintain sustained, rapid and sound development of the national economy

走出一条速度较快、效益较好、整体素质不断提高的经济协调发展的路子

find a way to coordinated development of the economy featuring a fairly high speed, fairly good performance and constant improvement of the quality of the economy as a whole

(一) 加强农业基础地位
Strengthening Agriculture as
the Foundation of the Economy

农业是国民经济的基础。

Agriculture is the foundation of the national economy.

农业、农村和农民问题是关系改革开放和现代化建设全局的重大问题。

The issues of agriculture, countryside and peasants (or agriculture, rural areas and farmers) are major issues having a bearing on the overall situation of China's reform, opening up and modernization.

必须始终把农业放在国民经济发展的首位。

We must always give first priority to agriculture in the development of the national economy.

必须始终把发展农村经济、提高农业生产力水平作为整个农村工作的中心。

We must always make the development of the rural economy and the raising of the level of agricultural productive forces the central task of all our rural work.

保持农业和农村经济的持续发展
maintain sustained development of agriculture and the rural economy

保持农民收入的稳定增长
ensure the steady increase of the peasants' income

保持农村社会的稳定
maintain social stability in rural areas

长期稳定党的农村基本政策
(1) keep the Party's basic rural policies stable for a long time to come
(2) stabilize the Party's basic rural policies over a long period of time

坚持以公有制为主体、多种所有制经济共同发展的基本经济制度
adhere to the basic economic system in which the public ownership is dominant and diverse types of ownership develop side by side

坚持以家庭承包经营为基础、统分结合的经营制度
adhere to the operation system of combining unification and separation, with the household contract operation as the basis

坚持以劳动所得为主和按生产要素分配相结合的分配制度
adhere to the distribution system that combines remuneration from one's work as the mainstay and remuneration according to essential factors of production put in

按照建立社会主义市场经济体制改革的要求，深化农村改革
deepen rural reform in accordance with the requirements for establishing a socialist market economy

实行家庭承包经营
practice household contract operation

稳定完善土地承包关系
stabilize and improve land contract relations

贯彻土地承包期再延长三十年的政策
carry out the policy of prolonging (or extending) the land contract period (or land contract term) for another 30 years

制定确保农村土地承包关系长期稳定的法律法规，赋予农民长期而有保障的土地使用权
make laws and statutes to ensure long-term stability of the rural land contract relations with a view to granting peasants a long-term and secure right to land-use

尊重农民的生产经营自主权
respect the decision-making power of peasants in their production and operations

调动广大农民的积极性
arouse (or mobilize) the enthusiasm (or initiative) of the broad masses of the peasants

保护农民的合法权益
protect the peasants' legitimate rights and interests

完善统分结合的双层经营体制
(1) improve the two-tier operation system that combines unified management with independent (or separate) management
(2) improve the two-tier management system that combines unification and separation (or diversification)
(3) improve two-layer management system featuring the integration of centralization and decentralization

逐步壮大集体经济实力
gradually boost the strength of the collective economy

在具备条件的地方，发展多种形式的土地适度规模经营
develop diverse forms of proper-scale land operation

where conditions are ripe

积极探索实现农业现代化的具体途径
try to explore concrete ways to realize the modernization of agriculture

发展农业产业化经营
promote an industrial management of agriculture

推动农产品生产、加工和销售环节的有机结合和相互促进
integrate the production, processing and marketing of farm produce and have all these sectors support each other

发展农工贸一体化
promote the integration of agriculture, industry and trade

推进农业向商品化、专业化、现代化的转变
give impetus to the development of agriculture toward commercialization, specialization and modernization

深化农产品流通体制改革
deepen the reform of circulation system for farm produce

完善农产品市场体系
improve the farm produce market system

改革粮棉购销体制,实行合理的价格政策
reform the grain and cotton purchasing and marketing system, and introduce a rational pricing policy

深化粮食流通体制改革
deepen the reform of the grain circulation (or distribution) system

建立粮食风险基金和粮食储备制度
set up a grain risk fund system and a grain reserve system

按保护价敞开收购农民余粮
purchase in an unlimited way the peasants' surplus grain at a protective price (or at protective prices)

加强农村商业网点建设

strengthen the building of a network of commercial establishments in rural areas

改革农业生产资料流通体制
reform the circulation system for means of agricultural production

积极开拓农村市场
take vigorous action to open up rural market

不放松粮食生产，积极发展多种经营
keep grain production high (or never slacken grain production) and actively develop a diversified economy

稳定发展粮食生产
steadily develop grain production

形成农村合理的产业结构
bring into being a rational industrial structure in rural areas

综合发展农林牧副渔各业
develop farming, forestry, animal husbandry, sideline production and fishery in an all-round way

提高农业综合生产能力
raise overall productivity in agriculture

确保农产品有效供给和农民收入持续增长
ensure an effective supply of farm produce and a sustained increase in peasants' income

实现农业可持续发展
achieve sustainable development in agriculture

多渠道增加农业投入
increase input in agriculture through multiple channels

加强农业基础设施建设
improve (or strengthen) agricultural infrastructure

加快以水利为重点的农业基本建设
accelerate agricultural capital construction focused on water conservancy projects

改善农业生产条件
better production conditions in agriculture

改善农业生态环境
improve ecological environment in (or for) agriculture

加强水利建设
(1) strengthen the construction of water conservancy facilities (or of water-control facilities)
(2) strengthen water conservancy construction
(3) make greater efforts to build water conservancy projects

加快大江大河大湖的治理
accelerate the harnessing of large rivers and lakes

提高防洪能力
(1) enhance the capability of preventing floods
(2) increase flood control

加强农田基本建设
(1) strengthen capital construction of (or on, or in) farmland
(2) strengthen the construction of farmland improvement projects

改造中低产田
transform medium- and low-yield fields

保护耕地、森林植被和水资源
protect farmland (or arable land, or cultivated land), forest vegetation and water resources

建立健全基本农田保护制度
set up and improve a system for protecting the basic farmland (or a basic farmland protection system)

在干旱地区发展节水灌溉和旱作农业
develop water-saving irrigation and dry-land farming in arid areas

大力推进科教兴农

step up the effort to develop agriculture by relying on science and education

农业的根本出路在科技、在教育。
The fundamental way out for agriculture lies in science, technology and education.

进行一次新的农业科技革命
carry on a new scientific and technological revolution in agriculture

大力推进农业科技进步
step up the effort to promote scientific and technological progress in agriculture

依靠科技进步，优化农业和农村经济结构
optimize the structure of agriculture and of the rural economy by relying on scientific and technological progress

提高科技对农业增长的贡献率
increase the contribution of science and technology to the growth in agriculture

推广先进适用技术
extend (or popularize) advanced and applicable techniques

实行科学种田
(1) practice scientific farming
(2) farm scientifically

提高农业机械化水平
(1) raise the level of mechanization of agriculture
(2) improve farm mechanization

提高农业集约经营水平
raise the level of intensive management of agriculture

发展高产优质高效农业和节水农业
develop an agriculture aimed at high yields, fine quality and high efficiency as well as good water-saving results

继续发展乡镇企业

continue to develop township enterprises (or township and village enterprises, or town and township enterprises)

积极推进乡镇企业改革

give a vigorous impetus to the reform of township enterprises

搞好小城镇规划建设

do well in planning and building up small towns and cities (or small towns)

发展和提高农村工业

develop and improve rural industry

结合小城镇建设发展第三产业

develop tertiary industry in combination with the construction of small towns and cities

多渠道转移农业富余劳动力

transfer surplus rural labor force through diversified channels

建立健全农业社会化服务体系

set up and improve a socialized service system for agriculture

办好供销合作社和信用合作社等农民合作经济组织

successfully run the peasants' economic cooperatives such as supply and marketing cooperatives and credit cooperatives

建立健全国家对农业的支持保护体系

set up and improve a state support and protection system for agriculture

坚持和完善"米袋子"省长负责制

uphold and improve the system of provincial governors assuming responsibility for the "rice bag"

坚持和完善"菜篮子"市长负责制

uphold and improve the system of city mayors assuming responsibility for the "vegetable basket"

根据农业的需要发展农用工业

develop the agroindustry in accordance with the needs of agriculture

切实减轻农民负担
(1) earnestly endeavor to lighten the burden on peasants
(2) really lighten the peasants' burdens

对农民要多予少取。
More should be given (to) and less taken from peasants.

(二) 调整和优化经济结构
Readjusting and Optimizing the Economic Structure

要对经济结构进行战略性调整。
We should make strategic readjustments in the economic structure.

以市场为导向,使社会生产适应国内外市场需求的变化
with the market as the orientation, make production respond to the changing demands of the domestic and foreign markets

依靠科技进步,促进产业结构优化
optimize the industrial structure by relying on scientific and technological progress

发挥各地优势,推动区域经济协调发展
promote coordinated development of regional economies by giving scope to the advantages in their respective localities

转变经济增长方式,改变高投入、低产出,高消耗、低效益的状况
change the mode of economic growth, putting an end to the situation featuring high input, low output, high consumption and low efficiency

全面提高国民经济整体素质和效益
(1) improve the quality and performance of the entire national economy in an all-round way
(2) improve the overall quality and performance of the

national economy in an all-round way

增强综合国力和国际竞争力
boost (or enhance) the overall national strength and international competitiveness

加强第一产业
strengthen the primary industry

调整和提高第二产业
readjust and upgrade the secondary industry

积极发展第三产业
vigorously develop the tertiary industry

改造和提高传统产业
transform and upgrade traditional industries

发展新兴产业和高技术产业
develop rising and high-tech industries

推进国民经济信息化
(1) give impetus to the extension of the use of information technology in national economy
(2) try to informationize the national economy

加强基础设施和基础工业(建设)
strengthen the construction of infrastructure and basic industries

加快发展水利、交通、通信、环保等基础设施和钢铁、能源等基础工业
accelerate the development of infrastructure including water conservancy, transportation (or communications), telecommunications and environmental protection and of the basic industries such as iron and steel and energy sectors

调整、改造加工工业
readjust and upgrade the processing industry

调整提高轻纺工业
readjust and improve (or upgrade) textile and other light industries

加强地质勘探
intensify geological exploration

振兴机械电子、石油化工、汽车制造和建筑业等支柱产业
invigorate pillar industries such as the machine building and electronics industries, the petrochemical industry, the automobile industry and construction industry (or building industry)

培育新的经济增长点
(1) cultivate new points of (or for) economic growth
(2) cultivate new economic growth points (or areas)

把开发新技术、新产品、新产业同开拓市场结合起来
combine the efforts to develop new technologies, products and industries with the efforts to open up markets

把发展技术密集型产业和劳动密集型产业结合起来
integrate the development of technology-intensive with labor-intensive industries

调整产品结构,提高产品质量
readjust the product mix and improve product quality

鼓励和引导第三产业加快发展
encourage and guide the tertiary industry so that it will develop at an accelerated pace

发展商业、金融、保险、旅游、信息、咨询、居民服务等第三产业
develop the tertiary industry including commerce, banking (or finance), insurance, tourism, information and consulting services and neighborhood services

引导房地产业健康发展
guide the real estate sector onto a path of sound development

促进地区经济合理布局和协调发展
promote rational distribution and coordinated development of regional economies

东部地区要在推进改革开放中实现更高水平的发展。

The eastern part of the country (or The eastern regions) should strive for a still higher level of development in the course of reform and opening up.

沿海发达地区要率先基本实现现代化。

The coastal developed regions should take the lead in achieving basic modernization.

中西部地区要加快改革开放和开发，发挥资源优势，发展优势产业。

The central and western parts of the country (or The central and western regions) should speed up the reform, opening up and development, make use of their advantages in natural resources, and develop related industries (or develop their superior industries, or develop their strong industries).

国家要加大对中西部地区的支持力度。

The state will increase its support for the central and western parts.

优先安排中西部地区的基础设施和资源开发项目

give the central and western parts priority in planning infrastructure and resources development projects.

鼓励国内外投资者到中西部地区投资

encourage both Chinese and overseas investors to invest in the central and western regions

发展东部地区同中西部地区多种形式的联合和合作

develop various forms of association and cooperation between the eastern and the central and western parts (or regions)

更加重视和积极帮助少数民族地区发展经济

pay more attention and give active support to areas inhabited by ethnic minorities in their economic development

逐步缩小地区发展差距

(1) minimize the regional development disparities step by step

(2) narrow the regional gap(s) in development step by step

(3) gradually narrow the gap(s) in development between different regions

发展各具特色的地区经济
develop regional economies with their respective characteristics

加快老工业基地的改造
speed up the upgrading of old industrial bases

发挥中心城市的作用
(1) let the central cities play their role
(2) give play to the role of the major cities

形成跨地区的经济区域和重点产业带
form (or establish) cross-regional economic zones and key industrial belts

以中心城市和交通要道为依托,形成和发展若干突破行政区划界限的经济区域
establish and develop a number of economic zones that transcend administrative boundaries, with major cities and vital communications lines as the basis

长江三角洲和整个长江流域地区
the Yangtze River Delta and the whole Yangtze River basin

环渤海地区
(1) the rim of Bohai Bay
(2) areas around the perimeter of Bohai Bay

东南沿海地区
the coastal region in southeast China

西南和华南部分省区(及重庆市)
some provinces and autonomous regions in southwest China (or in the Southwest) and South China (and Chongqing Municipality)

东北地区
northeast China (or the Northeast)

中部五省地区
region of the five provinces in the central part (Henan, Hubei, Hunan, Jiangxi and Anhui)

西北地区
northwest China (or the Northwest)

加快改革投融资体制
accelerate the reform of investment and financing systems

完善国家产业政策
improve state industrial policies

解决"大而全"、"小而全"和不合理重复建设问题
solve such problems as forming "large and all-inclusive" or "small and all-inclusive" units and launching irrational and duplicated construction projects

严格控制新开工项目
(1) strictly control the launching (or the start-up) of new projects
(2) make strict control over the launching of new projects

实行(建设)项目法人责任制
institute corporation (or legal person) responsibility system for (construction) projects

严格和完善项目资本金制度
strictly implement and improve the project capital system (or the capital funds system for projects)

逐步发展市场融资方式
gradually develop financing through the market (or develop market financing)

按照国家产业政策指导投资方向
guide investment direction in accordance with the state industrial policies

(三) 科教兴国战略
The Strategy of Developing the Country by Relying on Science and Education

科学技术是第一生产力。

Science and technology constitute a primary productive force.

当今世界,科技进步日新月异,知识经济正在兴起。

In the world of today, science and technology are progressing with each passing day and knowledge economy is unfolding.

科技进步是经济发展的决定性因素。

Scientific and technological progress is a decisive factor in economic development.

四个现代化,关键是科学技术现代化。

The key to the Four Modernizations is the modernization of science and technology.

科学技术人才的培养,基础在教育。

Education is basic to the training of scientific and technical personnel.

抓科技必须同时抓教育。

To promote scientific and technological work, it is necessary to improve education simultaneously.

实施科教兴国战略

(1) implement the strategy of developing the country by relying on science and education

(2) implement the strategy of revitalizing (or invigorating) the country through science and education

使经济建设转到依靠科技进步和提高劳动者素质的轨道上来

(1) get onto the path of developing our economy by relying on scientific and technological progress and improving the quality of laborers

(2) make economic development change to the track of depending on scientific and technological progress and improving the quality of laborers

(3) shift economic development to the path (or onto the track, or into the orbit) of relying on the advance of science and technology and improving the quality of workers

经济建设必须依靠科学技术,科学技术工作必须面向经济建设。

Economic development must rely on science and technology, and our work in science and technology must be adapted to the needs of economic development.

把加速科技进步放在经济社会发展的关键地位

make the acceleration of scientific and technological progress a vital task in economic and social development

提高科技进步对经济增长的贡献率

increase the contribution of scientific and technological progress to economic growth

制订科学发展规划要统观全局,突出重点,有所为、有所不为。

In drawing up science development programs, we should bear in mind the overall situation, highlight key areas, try to do certain things and refrain from doing other things.

加强基础性研究和高技术研究

strengthen basic research and research in high technology

加大发展高新技术的力度

redouble the efforts to develop high and new technology

发展高技术,加快实现高技术产业化

(1) develop high technology and accelerate the pace of applying high technology to production

(2) develop high technology and accelerate the industrialization of high-tech achievements

在世界高科技领域,中华民族要占有应有的位置。

The Chinese nation must take its place in the field of high

technology in the world.

迎接世界新技术革命的挑战

meet the challenge of the new technological revolution in the world

瞄准世界科技前沿，攀登科技高峰

(1) scale the heights of scientific and technological development in fields on the cutting edge of science and technology in the world

(2) aim at the world frontier sciences and technologies, and scale the heights in science and technology

重点发展新兴带头学科、交叉学科和应用基础学科

focus on the development of rising and leading disciplines, inter-disciplines and basic applied disciplines

加快电子信息、生物工程、新材料、新能源、海洋、环境和航天、航空等领域的研究开发

quicken the research and development of electronic information, bioengineering, new materials, new sources of energy, the ocean, the environment, astronautics, aeronautics and other fields

强化应用技术的开发和推广

intensify the development and spread of applied technologies

加强工农业技术开发

strengthen technological development in industry and agriculture

促进科技成果向现实生产力转化

promote the translation of scientific and technological achievements into practical (or actual, or real) productive forces

集中力量解决经济社会发展的重大和关键技术问题

concentrate on tackling major and key technological problems in economic and social development

办好国家高新技术产业开发区

run our national high and new technology industrial development zones well

广泛采用先进技术装备社会生产各部门

extensively adopt advanced technologies to equip various branches of (social) production

有重点有选择地引进先进技术

import advanced technologies from abroad with our priorities in mind and on a selective basis

自主开发和引进、消化先进技术相结合

combine development of technology through our own efforts with introduction and assimilation of overseas advanced technology

增强自主创新能力

(1) enhance the ability of independent innovation

(2) enhance our own abilities of independent creation

重视运用最新技术成果,实现技术发展的跨越

attach importance to the application of the latest technological achievements and bring about a leap in technological development (of our country)

深化科技和教育体制改革,促进科技、教育同经济的结合

deepen the reform of the management systems of science and technology and of education to promote the integration of science, technology and education with the economy

支持和鼓励企业从事科研、开发和技术改造

encourage and help enterprises to engage in research, development and technological upgrading (or technical transformation)

使企业成为科研开发和投入的主体

make enterprises the main force in research and development and the related investment

鼓励大型企业建立技术开发中心

encourage large enterprises to establish technology development centers

加强企业和科研院所、高等院校之间的联合

strengthen the association of enterprises with research academies, institutes and institutions of higher learning

有条件的科研机构和大专院校要以不同形式进入企业或同企业合作。

Wherever conditions permit, scientific research institutes and institutions of higher learning should enter into association or cooperation with enterprises in various ways.

走产学研结合的道路

(1) take the road of combining production, teaching and research

(2) take the road of combining productive units, educational institutions and research institutes

要鼓励创新、竞争和合作。

Innovation, competition and cooperation should be encouraged.

坚持创新,勇于创新

keep on and be brave in innovating (or creating and innovating)

创新是一个民族的灵魂,是一个国家兴旺发达的不竭动力。

Creativity is the soul of a nation and an inexhaustible source (or motive force) of a country's prosperity.

建设国家知识创新体系

institute a national knowledge innovation system

力争取得更多更大的科技创新成就

strive for more and greater scientific and technological innovations

实施保护知识产权制度

implement the regime of protecting intellectual property rights

建立一整套有利于人才培养和使用的激励机制
institute a whole set of incentive mechanisms favorable to the training and use of competent people (or talented personnel)

引进国外智力
(1) bring in intellectual resources from overseas
(2) introduce foreign intelligence
(3) recruit overseas intelligence

鼓励留学人员回国工作或以适当方式为祖国服务
encourage those studying abroad to return and work or render their service to the motherland in one way or another (or in an appropriate way)

积极开展国际间科学和教育的合作交流
actively develop international scientific and educational cooperation and exchanges

(四) 可持续发展战略
The Strategy of Achieving Sustainable Development

我国在现代化建设中必须实施可持续发展战略。
(1) Our country must implement the strategy of achieving sustainable development in the modernization drive.
(2) China must implement a sustainable development strategy in the modernization drive.

正确处理经济发展同人口、资源、环境的关系
(1) correctly handle the relationship of economic development versus (or with) population, natural resources and the environment
(2) correctly handle the relationship between economic development on the one hand and population, natural resources and the environment on the other

《中国二十一世纪议程——中国二十一世纪人口、环境与发展白皮书》
China's Agenda — White Paper on China's Population, Environment and Development in the 21st Century

坚持计划生育的基本国策
stick to the basic state policy of family planning

促进人口与经济、社会、资源、环境协调发展
promote a coordinated development between population on one hand and the economy, society, resources and environment on the other

中国实行计划生育坚持国家指导与群众自愿相结合的原则。
In the implementation of the family planning policy, China upholds a principle of combining state guidance with voluntary participation by the masses.

控制人口增长
control population growth

控制人口过快增长的重点在农村。
In controlling population overgrowth, the stress lies in rural areas.

提倡晚婚晚育
encourage late marriage and late childbirth

做好优生优育工作
(1) promote prenatal and postnatal care
(2) do a good job of bearing and rearing better children

提高人口素质
improve the population quality (or the quality of population)

儿童的生存、保护和发展是提高人口素质的基础。
Children's survival, protection and development are the basis for improving the quality of population.

重视人口老龄化问题
pay attention to the problem of an aging population (or the problem of the aging of population)

实现向低出生、低死亡、低自然增长的现代人口再生产类型的转变

bring about a transition to the modern population reproduction pattern characterized by a low birth rate, low death rate and low natural growth rate

保障自然资源的合理利用
ensure the rational use of natural resources

资源开发和节约并举,把节约放在首位,提高资源利用率。

(1) While exploiting our natural resources and making economical use of them, we lay emphasis on the latter so as to raise the efficiency of their utilization.

(2) We must exploit our natural resources and economize on them at the same time and give priority to practicing economy so as to raise the efficiency of the utilization of resources.

统筹规划国土资源开发和整治
make an overall plan for the development and improvement of our land and resources

加强对耕地、水、森林、草原、矿产、海洋、生物等资源的管理和保护

(1) tighten control over and protection (or conservation) of arable land, water, forest, grassland, mineral, marine, biological and other natural resources

(2) improve the management and protection of such resources as arable land, water, forests, grassland, minerals, seas and living beings

保护珍贵的动物和植物
protect rare animals and plants

合理开发和综合利用自然资源
rationally exploit our natural resources and make comprehensive use of them

实施资源有偿使用制度
institute a system of paid use of natural resources

坚持节水、节地、节能、节材、节粮以及节约各种资源
persist in economizing on (or saving on) water, land,

energy, materials, grain and all the other resources

实行适度消费政策
carry out a policy of proper consumption

坚持保护环境的基本国策
stick to the basic state policy of environmental protection

保护和改善生活环境和生态环境
protect and improve the living environment and the ecological environment

防治污染和其他公害
prevent and control pollution and other public hazards

坚持经济、社会和环境协调发展的方针
adhere to the principle of coordinated development between the economy, the society and the environment

经济建设、城乡建设和环境建设同步规划、同步实施、同步发展
（1）synchronizing the planning, implementation and progress of economic development, urban and rural construction and environmental protection
（2）simultaneous planning, simultaneous implementation and simultaneous development for economic construction, urban and rural construction and environmental construction

实现经济效益、社会效益、环境效益相统一
combine the economic returns with social effects and environmental benefits

普及环保知识
popularize environmental protection knowledge among the people

增强全民族环境意识
（1）enhance the whole nation's awareness of the importance of environmental protection
（2）raise the consciousness of the whole nation about environmental protection

— 66 —

健全环境保护的法律体系和管理体系

improve the law system and administrative system (or the legal and administrative systems) of environmental protection

加强对环境污染的治理

strengthen the control of environmental pollution

防治工业污染

prevent and control industrial pollution

实行"预防为主，防治结合"、"谁污染，谁治理"、"强化环境管理"三大政策

carry out three major policies of "putting prevention first and combining prevention with control", "making the causer of pollution responsible for treating it" and "intensifying environmental management"

实施污染物排放总量控制

enforce control over the totality of discharged pollutants

提高工业"三废"的处理能力

enhance the capability to treat the industrial "three wastes" (i.e. waste gas, waste water and waste residue)

提高工业"三废"综合利用率

raise the comprehensive utilization rate of the industrial "three wastes"

使用清洁能源，推行清洁生产

use clean energy and promote clean production

创造清洁高效的工艺

create clean and efficient technologies

防治噪声污染

prevent and control noise pollution

实行防止环境污染和破坏的设施与生产主体工程同时设计、同时施工、同时投产的制度

enforce a system in which facilities for preventing and controlling environmental pollution and destruction shall be designed, constructed and put into operation at the same time as the main production projects

结合技术改造防治工业污染
prevent and control industrial pollution in combination with technical transformation

对工业污染进行综合防治
carry out prevention and control of industrial pollution in a comprehensive way

开展城市环境综合整治
carry out comprehensive improvement of the urban environment

改善城市环境质量
improve the quality of the urban environment

公布大城市环境质量监测指标,促进环境质量的改善
publish standards for monitoring environmental quality in large cities with an aim to improving their environmental quality

国土整治和农村环境保护
territorial control and rural environmental protection

加强重点地区和重点流域污染的治理
strengthen the control of pollution in major regions and valleys

发展生态农业
develop eco-agriculture

控制农田污染和水污染
control farmland pollution and water pollution

植树种草
plant trees and grass

搞好水土保持
do well in the conservation of water and soil (or in water and soil conservation)

控制水土流失
control soil erosion

加强林业生态工程建设
strengthen the construction of forest ecological projects

防治荒漠化
prevent and control desertification

生物多样性保护
bio-diversity conservation

保护全球环境
protect the global environment

推进环境保护领域的国际合作
promote international cooperation in the field of environmental protection

实施中国海洋事业可持续发展战略
implement a sustainable development strategy for China's marine programs

《中国海洋二十一世纪议程》
China Ocean Agenda 21

合理开发利用海洋资源
rationally develop (or exploit) and utilize marine resources

保护和保全海洋环境
protect and preserve the marine environment

实现海洋资源、环境的可持续利用
realize the sustainable utilization of marine resources and marine environment

(四)提高对外开放水平
Doing Better in Opening to the Outside World

面对经济、科技全球化趋势,我们要以更加积极的姿态走向世界。

Confronted with globalization trends in economic, scientific and technological development, we should take an even more active stance in the world.

完善全方位、多层次、宽领域的对外开放格局
improve the pattern of opening up in all directions, at all levels and in a wide range

努力提高对外开放水平
(1) strive to do better in opening to the outside world
(2) strive to improve standard of opening to the outside world
(3) strive to raise the level of opening-up

要加强经济、科技、教育、文化等各个领域的国际交流与合作,努力提高开放的成效。
We should strengthen economic, scientific and technological, educational and cultural exchanges and cooperation with other countries and strive to do better in opening-up.

以提高效益为中心,努力扩大商品和服务的对外贸易,优化进出口结构。
Focusing on better results, we should strive to expand external trade in commodities and services and optimize the import and export mix.

积极开拓国际市场
vigorously open up markets abroad

坚持以质取胜和市场多元化战略
(1) stick to the strategy of achieving success on the strength of quality and a multi-outlet market
(2) stick to the strategy of success through quality and a multi-outlet market

进一步降低关税总水平,鼓励引进先进技术和关键设备
further lower the general level of tariffs and encourage the import of advanced technologies and key equipment

深化对外经济贸易体制改革

deepen the reform of the system of trade and economic relations with foreign countries

深化外贸体制改革
deepen the reform of the foreign trade system

完善代理制
improve the proxy system

扩大企业外贸经营权,形成平等竞争的政策环境
expand the power of enterprises to handle their own foreign trade so as to create a policy environment for competition on an equal footing

积极参与区域经济合作和全球多边贸易体系
take an active part in regional economic cooperation and the global system of multilateral trade

积极合理有效地利用外资
use foreign capital (or utilize foreign funds) actively, rationally and effectively

进一步改善国内投资环境
further improve China's investment environment

利用外资坚持重质量重效益的原则
stick to the principle of stressing the importance of quality and economic returns in the use of foreign capital

引导外资投向农业、基础设施、基础工业、高新技术产业和产品出口型项目
guide foreign investment toward agriculture, infrastructure, basic industries, high and new technology industries and export-oriented projects

鼓励外商投资项目更多地进入中西部地区
encourage foreign businessmen to further invest in the central and western parts of China

有步骤地推进服务业的对外开放
open the service industry (or service trades) to the outside world step by step

逐步开放金融、保险等服务领域

gradually open up finance (or banking), insurance and other fields of service

依法保护外商投资企业的权益,实行国民待遇,加强引导和监管。

In accordance with the law, we shall protect the rights and interests of foreign-funded enterprises, grant them the same treatment as their Chinese counterparts and improve guidance to and regulation of these enterprises.

鼓励能够发挥我国比较优势的对外投资

encourage Chinese investors to invest abroad in areas that can bring China's comparative advantages into play

更好地利用国内外两个市场、两种资源

make better use of both domestic (or Chinese) and foreign markets and resources

增强国际竞争力

enhance our international competitiveness

完善和实施涉外经济贸易的法律法规

improve and enforce laws and statutes governing China's trade and economic relations with foreign countries

保持国际收支平衡

maintain an equilibrium in the international balance of payments

保持人民币汇率稳定

keep stable the exchange rates for the Renminbi (RMB) against other currencies

进一步办好经济特区和上海浦东新区

(1) better operate the special economic zones and the Pudong New Area in Shanghai

(2) do better in running the special economic zones and the Pudong New Area of Shanghai

(六)改善人民生活
Improving the Standard of Living of the People

提高人民生活水平,是改革开放和发展经济的根本目的。

Raising the standard of living of the people is the fundamental goal of the reform, opening up and economic development.

在经济发展的基础上努力增加城乡居民实际收入

try to increase the real income of the residents in both urban and rural areas on the basis of economic growth

拓宽消费领域,引导合理消费

broaden the range of consumption with proper guidance

改善人民的物质生活

improve the people's material well-being

充实人民的精神生活

enrich the people's cultural life

美化生活环境

beautify the living environment

提高生活质量

enhance (or improve) the quality of life

特别要改善居住、卫生、交通和通信条件,扩大服务性消费。

Special efforts should be made to improve housing, sanitation, transportation and communication conditions and expand the range of service consumption.

把解决居民住房问题放在突出位置

give priority to the solution of the housing problem for the residents

加快"安居工程"建设

accelerate the construction of "adequate (or comfortable)

housing projects"

增加公共设施和社会福利设施
build more public and social welfare facilities

发展社区服务
expand community services

提高教育和医疗保健水平
improve the level of education and medical and health care

实行保障城镇困难居民基本生活的政策
adopt a policy that ensures the basic standard of living for urban residents in difficulty

建立城市贫困居民的最低生活保障制度
institute a system for ensuring a minimum standard of living for impoverished urban residents

重视老龄和残疾人工作
attach importance to work for the aged and the disabled

扶贫
(1) assist poverty-stricken people (or indigent people)
(2) assist poverty-stricken areas (or poor areas)
(3) help the poor
(4) aid-the-poor

加大扶贫攻坚力度
(1) make greater efforts to fight poverty
(2) intensify the work of fighting poverty
(3) step up our efforts to assist indigent people

做好扶贫开发工作
make a good job of anti-poverty development

解决农村贫困人口的温饱问题
provide adequate food and clothing for impoverished people in rural areas

脱贫致富
shake off poverty and become prosperous

加强自然灾害的监测预报和防治

intensify preventing and controlling as well as monitoring and forecasting of the natural disasters

做好抗灾救灾工作

make a good job of fighting disasters and disaster relief

千方百计安排好灾区人民生活，帮助他们生产自救

try every possible means to make adequate arrangements for the people in disaster areas and help them to restore normal life through their own production

七、政治体制改革和民主法制建设
Political Restructuring and the Development of Democracy and the Legal System

（一）建设有中国特色的社会主义民主政治
Building a Socialist Democracy with Chinese Characteristics

我们的政治体制改革，目标是建设有中国特色的社会主义民主政治。

The goal of the reform of the political structure is to build a socialist democracy with Chinese characteristics.

发展社会主义民主
develop socialist democracy

健全社会主义法制
improve (or perfect) the socialist legal system

依法治国
(1) manage (or administer, or run) state affairs according to law
(2) govern (or administer) the country according to law
(3) rule the country by law

建设社会主义法治国家
build a socialist country ruled by law

发展社会主义民主政治，是中国共产党始终不渝的奋斗目标。

It is a persistent goal of the Communist Party of China to develop socialist democracy.

没有民主就没有社会主义，就没有社会主义现代化。

Without democracy there would be no socialism or socialist modernization.

社会主义民主的本质是人民当家作主。

The essence of socialist democracy is that the people are the masters of the country.

中华人民共和国的一切权力属于人民。

All power in the People's Republic of China belongs to the people.

中华人民共和国国家机构实行民主集中制的原则。

The state organs of the People's Republic of China apply the principle of democratic centralism.

坚持和完善我国的根本政治制度——人民民主专政的国体和人民代表大会制度的政体

uphold and improve China's fundamental political system, which is constituted of the state system featuring the people's democratic dictatorship and the system of government featuring the people's congresses

造成又有集中又有民主，又有纪律又有自由，又有统一意志、又有个人心情舒畅、生动活泼，那样一种政治局面

create a political situation in which we have (or in which there are) both centralism and democracy, both discipline and freedom, both unity of will and personal ease of mind and liveliness

发展民主必须同健全法制紧密结合。

(1) Developing democracy must go hand in hand with the efforts to improve the legal system.

(2) Developing democracy must be closely integrated with the improvement of the legal system.

依法治国是党领导人民治理国家的基本方略。

Ruling the country by law is the basic strategy employed by the Party in leading the people in running the country.

依法治国把坚持党的领导、发扬人民民主和严格依法办事统一起来。

In ruling the country by law, we can unify the adherence to Party leadership, the development of the people's democracy and doing things in strict accordance with the law.

推进政治体制改革
press ahead with the reform of the political structure (or with political restructuring)

增强党和国家的活力
enhance the vitality of the Party and the state

保持和发挥社会主义制度的特点和优势
retain and demonstrate the features and advantages of the socialist system

维护国家统一、民族团结和社会稳定
safeguard the unification of the country, the unity of the nationalities and social stability

充分发挥人民群众的积极性
give full scope to the initiative of the masses

促进生产力发展和社会进步
stimulate the development of productive forces and social progress

(二)健全民主制度
Improving the Systems of Democracy

社会主义建设事业必须依靠工人、农民和知识分子,必须依靠各民族人民的团结,必须依靠全体社会主义劳动者、拥护社会主义的爱国者和拥护祖国统一的爱国者的最广泛的统一战线。

In building socialism it is essential to rely on the workers, peasants and intellectuals, on the unity of the people of various nationalities, and on the broadest united front of all socialist working people, all patriots who support socialism and all patriots who stand for the reunification of the motherland.

中国共产党领导和支持人民掌握管理国家的权力。

The Communist Party of China leads and supports the people in exercising the power of running the state.

实行民主选举、民主决策、民主管理、民主监督

hold democratic elections, make policy decisions in a democratic manner, institute democratic management and supervision

保证人民依法享有广泛的权利和自由

ensure that the people enjoy extensive rights and freedom endowed by law

尊重和保障人权

respect and guarantee human rights

中国将人民的生存权和发展权置于首位。

China places top priority on its people's rights to subsistence and development.

坚持和完善人民代表大会制度

uphold and improve the system of the people's congresses (or the people's congress system)

保证人民代表大会及其常委会依法履行国家权力机关的职能,加强立法和监督工作

ensure that the people's congresses and their standing committees exercise the functions of the organs of state power according to law, and strengthen their legislative and supervisory work

密切人民代表同人民的联系

establish closer ties between deputies and the people they represent

要把改革和发展的重大决策同立法结合起来。

It is necessary to integrate major policy decisions concerning reform and development with legislation.

保证决策科学化、民主化

ensure that decision-making (process) is more scientific and democratic

坚持和完善共产党领导的多党合作和政治协商制度

uphold and improve the system of multi-party cooperation and political consultation led by (or under the leadership of) the Communist Party

坚持"长期共存、互相监督、肝胆相照、荣辱与共"的方针

uphold the principle of "long-term coexistence, mutual supervision, treating each other with all sincerity and sharing weal or woe"

加强共产党同民主党派的合作共事

strengthen the cooperation of the Communist Party with the democratic parties

巩固共产党同党外人士的联盟

consolidate the alliance of the Communist Party with non-Party people

继续推进人民政协政治协商、民主监督、参政议政的规范化、制度化

continue to help the people's political consultative conferences to standardize and institutionalize their political consultation, democratic supervision, participation in and deliberation of state affairs

使人民政协成为共产党团结各界的重要渠道

turn the people's political consultative conferences into an important channel for the Communist Party to unite with people from all circles

巩固和发展广泛的爱国统一战线

consolidate and develop a broad patriotic united front

全面贯彻党的民族政策

implement in an all-round way the Party's policies toward ethnic minorities (or the Party's policy toward nationalities)

坚持和完善民族区域自治制度

(1) uphold and improve the system of regional autonomy in areas inhabited by ethnic minorities (or minority nationali-

ties)

(2) uphold and improve the system of regional autonomy of minority nationalities

(3) uphold and improve regional national autonomy system

巩固和发展平等、团结、互助的社会主义民族关系
consolidate and develop (or enhance) socialist relations of equality, unity and mutual assistance among the nationalities

加快发展少数民族地区的经济和科学文化事业
accelerate the economic, scientific and cultural development in the minority nationality regions (or ethnic minority regions)

促进各民族共同繁荣进步
promote common prosperity and progress for all our nationalities

认真贯彻党的宗教政策
implement in real earnest the Party's policy concerning religion

保障公民宗教信仰自由
safeguard citizens' freedom of religious belief

引导宗教与社会主义社会相适应
help various religions adapt to socialist society

认真贯彻党的侨务政策
implement in real earnest the Party's policy concerning overseas Chinese affairs

保护华侨的正当的权利和利益,保护归侨和侨眷的合法的权利和利益
protect the legitimate rights and interests of Chinese nationals residing abroad and protect the lawful rights and interests of returned overseas Chinese and of the family members of overseas Chinese

工会、共青团、妇联等群众团体要在管理国家和社会事务中发挥民主参与和民主监督作用,成为党联系广大

人民群众的桥梁和纽带。

The trade unions, the Communist Youth League, the women's federations and other mass organizations should play their role of democratic participation and supervision in managing state and social affairs (or in administering state affairs and managing social affairs), and serve as a bridge and bond linking the Party with the broad masses of the people.

扩大基层民主

extend the scope of democracy at the grassroots level

加强基层民主建设

(1) strengthen (or improve) democracy at the grassroots level

(2) improve grassroots democracy

城乡基层政权机关和基层群众性自治组织都要健全民主制度。

The grassroots organs of power and self-governing mass organizations in both urban and rural areas should improve the systems of democracy.

健全民主选举制度

(1) improve the system of democratic elections

(2) establish a sound system of democratic elections

实行政务和财务公开

keep the public informed of the political activities and financial affairs

让群众参与讨论和决定基层公共事务和公益事业，对干部实行民主监督

enable the masses to take a direct part in the discussion and decision-making concerning public affairs and welfare undertakings at the grassroots level, and exercise supervision over the cadres

完善城镇居民自治制度

improve the system of self-government of urban residents

城市居民委员会

（urban）neighborhood committee

完善农村村民自治制度
improve the system of self-government of villagers（or village people）

村民委员会
villagers' committee（or village committee）

坚持和完善企事业民主管理制度
uphold and improve the democratic management system of enterprises and institutions

职工代表大会
(1) congress of workers and（office）staff
(2) workers' conference

（三）加强法制建设
Improving the Legal System

有法可依,有法必依,执法必严,违法必究。
(1) There must be laws to go by, the laws must be observed and strictly enforced, and law-breakers must be prosecuted.
(2) There shall be laws to abide by, everyone should abide by the law, the law must be enforced strictly, and those who violate the law must be dealt with.

加强立法工作,提高立法质量
strengthen legislation and improve its quality

形成有中国特色社会主义法律体系
form a socialist legal system with Chinese characteristics

建立社会主义市场经济法律体系
establish a law system（or legal system）for socialist market economy

维护宪法和法律的尊严
safeguard the dignity（or sanctity）of the Constitution and other laws

严格执行宪法和法律

enforce the Constitution and other laws strictly

坚持法律面前人人平等

see to it that all people are equal before the law

一切政府机关都必须依法行政。

All government organs must perform their official duties according to law.

切实保障公民权利

guarantee the citizens' rights in real earnest

推进司法改革,从制度上保证司法机关依法独立公正地行使审判权和检察权

promote the reform of judicial affairs to ensure institutionally that the judicial organs are in a position to exercise adjudicative and procuratorial power independently and fairly according to law

建立冤案、错案责任追究制度

establish a system for investigating and prosecuting anyone who is held responsible for unjust or misjudged cases

加强执法和司法队伍建设

improve the ranks of law-enforcing and judicial personnel

开展普法教育,增强全民的法律意识

educate the populace about the law to make them more aware of its importance

着重提高领导干部的法制观念和依法办事能力

enhance in particular the leading cadres' awareness of the importance of the legal system and their ability to perform their duties according to law

法制建设同精神文明建设紧密结合、同步推进

closely integrate the improvement of the legal system with the promotion of cultural and ideological progress and make sure that they advance synchronously

(四)推进机构改革
Reforming the Structure of Government Institutions

积极推进政府机构改革
(1) actively reform the structure of government institutions
(2) actively restructure government institutions

转变政府职能
alter the functions of the government

实现政企分开
separate the functions of the government from those of enterprises

根据精简、统一、效能的原则进行机构改革
reform the structure of government institutions in line with the principle of simplification, uniformity and efficiency

建立办事高效、运转协调、行为规范的行政管理体系
establish a highly efficient, well-coordinated and standardized administrative system

提高为人民服务的水平
improve the service for the people

加强宏观调控部门和执法监管部门
reinforce departments handling macroeconomic control and those supervising law enforcement

培育和发展社会中介组织
cultivate and expand social intermediary organizations

深化行政体制改革
deepen the reform of the administrative system

加强行政组织立法,实现各级政府机构、职能、编制的法制化
strengthen legislation relating to administrative institutions in order to statutorily delimit the structures, functions and sizes of governments at all levels

深化人事制度改革
deepen the reform of the personnel system

引入竞争激励机制
introduce a competitive and incentive mechanism

完善(国家)公务员制度
(1) improve the system of public servants (or of public service)
(2) improve the civil service system

建设一支高素质的专业化国家行政管理干部队伍
build (up) a contingent of administrators who are highly competent and professionally specialized

所有政府工作人员都要做人民满意的公务员。
All government functionaries should become public servants with whom the people are satisfied.

(五)完善民主监督制度
Improving the System of Democratic Supervision

一切干部都是人民的公仆,必须受到人民和法律的监督。
All cadres are the people's servants who must be subjected to supervision by the people and the law.

完善监督法制
improve the legal system of supervision

建立健全依法行使权力的制约机制
(1) establish and improve a mechanism ensuring that our cadres exercise their authority within the framework of law
(2) establish and perfect a restrictive mechanism for ensuring that the power is exercised according to law

坚持公平、公正、公开的原则,直接涉及群众切身利益的部门要实行公开办事制度。
The departments handling affairs of immediate concern to the masses should carry out an open administrative system to make sure what they do is fair, just and open.

把党内监督、法律监督、群众监督结合起来
integrate the supervision by Party members (or the inner-Party supervision) with the supervision by the law and the masses

发挥舆论监督的作用
give scope to the role of supervision by public opinion

加强对宪法和法律实施的监督
strengthen the supervision over the enforcement of the Constitution and other laws

维护国家法制统一
safeguard the uniformity of the legal system of the state

加强对党和国家方针政策贯彻的监督,保证政令畅通
strengthen the supervision over the implementation of general and specific policies (or of the principles and policies) of the Party and the state to see to it that they are truly carried out

加强对各级干部特别是领导干部的监督
strengthen the supervision over cadres at all levels and especially leading cadres

防止(干部)滥用权力
prevent cadres from abusing their power

严惩执法犯法、贪赃枉法
severely punish those in charge of law enforcement who break the law and those who accept bribes

（六）维护安定团结
Maintaining Stability and Unity

各级党委和政府必须认真负责、满腔热情地解决人民群众生活和工作中的实际问题。
The Party committees and governments at all levels must work conscientiously, responsibly and enthusiastically to solve the practical problems in the life and work of the masses.

正确处理人民内部矛盾

correctly handle the contradictions among the people

搞好社会治安
(1) make a good job of public security
(2) ensure that public order is sound

强化人民民主专政职能
strengthen (the functions of) the people's democratic dictatorship

加强政法工作
improve the work of the procuratorial, judicial and public security departments

依法严厉打击各种犯罪活动
severely crack down on all kinds of crime (or crack down on various criminal activities) according to law

坚决扫除黄赌毒等社会丑恶现象
resolutely eradicate social evils such as pornography, gambling, and drug abuse and trafficking

加强社会治安综合治理
improve all facets of public security

创造良好的社会治安环境
bring about a sound environment for public security

维护国家安全和社会稳定
safeguard national security and social stability

确保国家长治久安
(1) guarantee the long-term (peace and) stability of the country
(2) guarantee the lasting political stability of the country
(3) ensure long-term security and order for the state

巩固和发展全国人民的大团结
consolidate and develop the great unity of the people of the whole country

八、有中国特色社会主义的文化建设
Developing Socialist Culture with Chinese Characteristics

只有经济、政治、文化协调发展,只有物质文明和精神文明都搞好,才是有中国特色社会主义。

Only when economic development and political and cultural advances are well coordinated and only if there are both material progress and cultural and ideological progress can there be socialism with Chinese characteristics.

社会主义现代化应该有繁荣的经济,也应该有繁荣的文化。

Socialist modernization requires both a prosperous economy and a flourishing culture.

有中国特色社会主义的文化,是凝聚和激励全国各族人民的重要力量,是综合国力的重要标志。

A socialist culture with Chinese characteristics is a major force in uniting and inspiring the people of all our nationalities, and an important indicator of our overall national strength.

提高全民族的思想道德素质和科学文化素质
(1) improve the ideological and ethical quality and the scientific and cultural quality of the whole nation
(2) raise the ideological and ethical standards and scientific and educational levels of the whole nation

为经济发展和社会全面进步提供强大的精神动力和智力支持

provide a powerful ideological driving force and strong intellectual support for economic development and all-round social progress

培育适应社会主义现代化要求的一代又一代有理想、有道德、有文化、有纪律的公民

nurture citizens one generation after another who have high ideals (or lofty ideals), moral integrity, a good education and a strong sense of discipline, meeting the requirements of the socialist modernization drive

(一)思想道德建设
Ideological and Ethical Progress

在全社会形成共同理想和精神支柱,是有中国特色社会主义文化建设的根本。

Fostering common ideals and aspirations in the whole society is the basic objective of (or is of fundamental importance for) our cultural advancement with Chinese characteristics.

要始终不渝地用邓小平理论教育干部和群众。

We should make unremitting efforts to educate cadres and the masses in Deng Xiaoping Theory.

开展以为人民服务为核心、集体主义为原则的社会主义道德教育

conduct education in socialist ethics focused on serving the people and based on the principle of collectivism

提倡爱祖国、爱人民、爱劳动、爱科学、爱社会主义

(1) advocate love of the motherland, of the people, of labor, of science and of socialism

(2) advocate love for the motherland, the people, labor, science and socialism

加强社会公德、职业道德、家庭美德建设

(1) vigorously advance progress in social morality (or public morality, or social ethics), professional ethics and family virtues

(2) promote progress in social, occupational and family ethics

在全社会形成团结互助、平等友爱、共同前进的人际关系

form in all aspects of society a relationship among people (or an interpersonal relationship) that is characterized by unity and mutual help, equality and affection and common progress

加强民主法制教育和纪律教育
strengthen education in democracy and the legal system (or in democracy and legality) and education in discipline

引导人们树立正确的世界观、人生观、价值观
guide people to foster a correct outlook on the world and life and correct values (or foster correct world outlook, outlook on life and values)

坚持爱国主义、集体主义、社会主义教育
adhere to education in patriotism, collectivism and socialism

弘扬爱国主义、集体主义、社会主义和艰苦创业精神
promote patriotism, collectivism, socialism and the hardworking and enterprising (or hardworking and pioneering) spirit

进行中国近代史、现代史、中共党史和基本国情教育
conduct education about China's modern and contemporary history (or the history of modern and contemporary China), the history of the Communist Party of China and the basic national conditions

在全社会发扬自尊、自信、自强的民族精神
enhance in the whole society the national spirit of self-respect, self-confidence and self-reliance (or self-support)

以贡献全部力量建设和保卫社会主义祖国为最大光荣,以损害社会主义祖国利益、尊严和荣誉为最大耻辱
(1) deem it the highest honor to contribute all to building and defending our socialist motherland, and deem it the deepest disgrace to impair her interest, dignity or honor
(2) regard utter devotion to building and defending the socialist motherland as the greatest glory, and damage to her interests, dignity or honor as the greatest shame

牢固树立勤俭建国、勤俭办一切事业的思想

firmly establish the concept of building our country and doing everything through diligence and thrift

发扬艰苦奋斗精神

promote the spirit of hard struggle (or hard work)

弘扬伟大的抗洪精神

carry forward the great spirit of flood-fighting

提倡共产主义思想道德

advocate communist ideology and ethics

鼓励一切有利于国家统一、民族团结、经济发展、社会进步的思想道德

encourage all ideologies and ethics that are conducive to unification of our country, unity of the nationalities, economic development and social progress

发扬社会主义的人道主义精神

carry forward socialist humanitarianism

要十分重视青少年思想道德建设。

We should pay great attention to ideological and ethical progress of young people (or of the youth and youngsters).

帮助青少年树立远大理想，培育优良品德

help young people foster lofty ideals and nurture fine moral character

反对和抵制拜金主义、享乐主义和个人主义

oppose and resist money worship (or the worship of money), hedonism (or pleasure seeking) and individualism

反对小团体主义、本位主义

oppose petty cliquism (or small group mentality) and departmental selfishness

反对损公肥私、损人利己

oppose seeking private gain at public expense and harming others to benefit oneself

纠正损害群众利益的部门和行业不正之风

rectify unsound practices (or correct unhealthy tendencies) in departments and trades that harm the interests of the masses

抵御资本主义和封建主义腐朽思想的侵蚀
resist the corrosion of decadent capitalist and feudal (or feudalistic) ideas (or ideologies)

(二)教育和科学
Education and Science

发展教育和科学,是文化建设的基础工程。
The progress of education and science is the foundation of our cultural advancement.

必须把教育摆在优先发展的战略地位。
We must make (or give) education a strategic priority.

培养同现代化要求相适应的数以亿计的高素质的劳动者和数以千万计的专门人才
train hundreds of millions of qualified laborers and tens of millions of professional personnel suited to the requirements of the modernization drive

发挥我国巨大人力资源的优势
exploit the advantage of the vast human resources of our country

教育要面向现代化,面向世界,面向未来。
(1) Education should be geared to the needs of modernization, of the world and of the future.
(2) We should orient our education work to the needs of modernization, the world and the future.

教育必须为社会主义现代化建设服务,必须与生产劳动相结合。
Education must serve socialist modernization drive and be combined with productive labor.

坚持教育的社会主义方向
adhere to the socialist orientation in education

认真贯彻党的［国家的］教育方针

implement in earnest the Party's［the state's］educational policy

培养德智体（等）全面发展的社会主义事业的建设者和接班人

(1) train builders of and successors to the cause of socialism, who are developed morally, intellectually and physically in an all-round way

(2) train builders of and successors to the cause of socialism with an all-round development in moral, intellectual and physical and other aspects

继续推进教育的改革和发展

continue to promote the reform and development of education

加强基础教育

strengthen basic education

普及九年义务教育

make the nine-year compulsory education universal

扫除青壮年文盲

eliminate illiteracy among young and middle-aged people

积极发展中等、高等职业教育和成人教育

actively expand secondary, higher vocational and adult education

开展多种形式的岗位和技术培训

conduct many forms of on-the-job and technical training

稳步发展高等教育

steadily develop higher education

集中力量办好一批重点大学和重点学科

concentrate on a number of key universities and key disciplines and specialties

完善研究生培养和学位制度

improve the system of training graduate students and the

academic degree system

重视和扶持少数民族地区的教育事业
attach importance to and support educational development in the ethnic minority areas

重视发展残疾人教育事业
attach importance to developing education for the disabled

优化教育结构
optimize the educational structure

加快高等教育管理体制改革步伐
speed up the reform of the management system of higher education

合理配置教育资源
judiciously allocate resources for education

提高教育[教学]质量和办学效益
(1) enhance the quality of education [instruction] and raise the overall efficiency of schools
(2) improve the quality of education [instruction] and the efficiency in running schools

改革办学体制
reform the system of running schools

鼓励社会力量办学
encourage non-governmental sectors to run schools

逐步形成政府办学为主与社会参与办学的新体制
gradually establish a new educational system in which the government dominates and different sectors of society participate in the running of schools

改革高等学校招生制度和缴费制度
reform the enrollment system and tuition system of institutions of higher learning (or universities and colleges)

改革高等学校毕业生就业制度
reform the employment system for graduates from institu-

tions of higher learning (or universities and colleges)

完善助学金、奖学金、贷学金制度
improve the stipend system, scholarship system and the system for student loans

组织勤工俭学
organize work-study programs

重视受教育者素质的提高
pay great attention to improving the quality of students (or the quality of everyone who receives an education)

基础教育由"应试教育"向素质教育转变
(1) shift the basic education from "education for examination" to education for improving the quality of students
(2) shift the basic education from examination-dominated education to quality-oriented one

实施全面素质教育
conduct education with emphasis on improving the overall quality of students

加强和改进德育工作
strengthen and improve work in moral education

加强和改善思想品德课程和政治理论课程
consolidate and improve courses in ideology and moral character and courses in political theory

改革教学内容、课程体系和教学方法
reform the content of courses (or course content), the curriculum and teaching methods

加强基本知识、基础理论和基本技能的培养和训练
improve the training of students in elementary knowledge, basic theories and basic skills

培养学生分析问题和解决问题的能力
develop the students' ability to analyze and solve problems

培养学生的创新能力

develop the students' ability to innovate (or to create)

促进教学、科研、生产三结合
promote three-in-one combination of teaching, research and production

加强和改善学校的体育卫生工作
strengthen and improve work in physical education and school hygiene

加强美育
improve aesthetic education

发挥美育在教育教学中的作用
give play to the role of aesthetic education in teaching and in education as a whole

组织学生参加生产劳动和社会实践
organize students to take part in productive labor and social practice

进行教育质量的评估和检查
carry on assessment of and check-up for educational quality

改革和完善教育投资体系，多渠道增加教育投入
reform and improve the system for investment in education to increase input through various channels

坚持以国家财政拨款为主，多渠道筹措教育经费
adhere to raising educational funds (or expenditures) through multiple channels with the state's financial allocation as the mainstay

尊师重教
(1) respect teachers and prize (or value) education
(2) respect teachers and their teaching

加强师资队伍建设
strengthen (or improve) the ranks of teachers

改善教师的工作和生活条件
improve teachers' working and living conditions

发展自然科学和社会科学事业
promote the development of the natural (sciences) and social sciences

提高科学技术水平
raise the scientific and technological level

普及科学和技术知识
(1) popularize science and technology
(2) disseminate knowledge of science and technology

引导人们树立科学精神, 掌握科学方法
guide people to take a scientific approach and master scientific methods

鼓励发明创造
encourage people to be creative and inventive (or to create and invent)

奖励科学研究成果和技术发明创造
commend and reward achievements in scientific research as well as technological innovations and inventions

消除愚昧, 反对封建迷信活动
eliminate ignorance and combat feudal and superstitious activities

迎接知识经济时代
greet an era of knowledge economy

建设国家创新体系
build a state innovation system

增强科技创新能力
(1) enhance the scientific and technological innovating capacity
(2) enhance the capacity for scientific and technological innovation

建立和发展中国自己的高技术产业
establish and develop China's own high-tech industries

在社会生产、流通、消费和环境保护等领域, 大力推

广先进适用技术

strive to propagate the use of applicable advanced technologies (or advanced and applicable techniques) for production, distribution, consumption, environmental protection and other fields

促进科技成果尤其是信息技术成果的商品化

promote the commercialization of scientific and technological achievements, and especially advances in information technology

完善社会化科技服务体系

improve scientific and technological services for society

发展哲学、社会科学

develop philosophy and (other) social sciences

坚持马克思主义在我国意识形态领域的指导地位

retain the guiding position of Marxism in the ideological sphere of our country

探索有中国特色社会主义的发展规律

study the laws governing the development of socialism with Chinese characteristics

增强我们认识世界、改造世界的能力

improve our ability to understand the world and change it

哲学社会科学必须坚持以马克思列宁主义、毛泽东思想、邓小平理论为指导。

Philosophy and social sciences must adhere to the guidance of Marxism-Leninism, Mao Zedong Thought and Deng Xiaoping Theory.

哲学社会科学必须坚持理论联系实际,为党和政府决策服务,为两个文明建设服务。

Philosophy and social sciences must keep to linking theory and (or with) practice, and serve the decision-making of the Party and government as well as the promotion of material progress and cultural and ideological progress.

坚持百家争鸣的方针,促进科学进步

adhere to the principle (or policy) of letting a hundred schools of thought contend, promoting progress in the sciences

(三)文学艺术、新闻出版、广播影视
Literature and Art, the Press and Publishing, Radio, Film and Television

发展文学艺术、新闻出版、广播影视等事业,是文化建设的重要内容。

The development of the cultural undertakings, including literature and art, the press and publishing, radio, film and television, is an important aspect of cultural advancement.

繁荣文学艺术
(1) enable literature and art to flourish
(2) promote flourishing literature and art
(3) boost literature and art

坚持为人民服务、为社会主义服务的方向
keep to the orientation (or adhere to the principle) of serving the people and the cause of socialism (or serving the people and socialism)

贯彻百花齐放、百家争鸣的方针
carry out the principle of letting a hundred flowers blossom and a hundred schools of thought contend

弘扬主旋律,提倡多样化
give full scope to the theme of our times while advocating diversity

树立精品意识,实施精品战略
foster the awareness of and implement a strategy of creating excellent works

创作出更多思想性和艺术性统一的优秀作品
create more excellent works which integrate ideological content with artistry

人民需要文艺,文艺更需要人民。

The people need literature and art, while literature and art need the people even more.

文艺工作者要深入群众，深入生活，汲取营养，丰富自己。

Writers and artists should get nutrition, and enrich themselves by immersing themselves among the masses, and by plunging into the thick of life.

文艺工作者要树立正确的创作思想。

Writers and artists should have correct creative ideas (or correct ideas guiding creation).

把最好的精神食粮贡献给人民

(1) provide the people with the best mental nourishment

(2) contribute the best nourishment for the mind to the people

尊重文艺创作规律

respect the law of literary and artistic creation

充分发挥文艺工作者的创造精神

give full play to the creativity of writers and artists

使不同的艺术风格和艺术形式得以自由发展

let different art styles and art forms develop freely

开展健康的文艺批评

carry out healthy literary or art criticism

新闻宣传必须坚持党性原则，坚持实事求是，把握正确的舆论导向。

In publicity (or propaganda) work, the press must adhere to the principle of keeping the Party spirit, persist in seeking truth from facts and maintain a correct orientation for public opinion.

对新闻出版业要加强管理，优化结构，提高质量。

It is necessary to tighten control over the press and publishing, optimizing their structures and improving their quality.

党报、党刊、国家通讯社和电台、电视台要发挥主导作用。

The newspapers and journals of the Chinese Communist Party, the state news agency and radio and television stations should play a leading role.

着力提高出版物质量

endeavor to improve the quality of the publications

及时反映国内外新的优秀文化成果

demonstrate in time outstanding Chinese and foreign cultural achievements

重视出版传统文化精品和有价值的学术著作

pay attention to the publishing of traditional excellent cultural works and valuable academic works

广播电视要努力提高节目质量。

The broadcasting and television stations should endeavor to improve the quality of their programs.

正确使用祖国语言文字

correctly use the spoken and written language of the motherland

深化文化体制改革

deepen the reform of the system for managing cultural undertakings

落实和完善文化经济政策

implement and improve the economic policies relating to cultural undertakings

(四)卫生和体育
Public Health and Sports

发展卫生体育事业,提高国民身体素质

promote public health and sports and improve people's (or national) physical fitness

推进卫生体育事业的改革和发展

promote the reform and development of public health and

sports

坚持为人民健康服务、为社会主义现代化服务的方向

keep to the orientation of serving the people's health and the socialist modernization

实现卫生事业同经济、社会协调发展

achieve a coordinated development between public health and the economy and society

做到人人享有卫生保健

manage to ensure that health care is provided for everyone

把卫生工作的重点放在农村

place emphasis on rural areas in public health

实行预防为主的方针

carry out the principle of giving priority to the prevention of diseases

加强对常见病、传染病、地方病、职业病的防治工作

strengthen the prevention and treatment of common, contagious, endemic and occupational diseases

中西医并重

attach equal importance to traditional Chinese medicine and western medicine

发展中医药事业

develop traditional Chinese medicine and pharmacology

依靠科技进步发展卫生事业

develop public health by relying on scientific and technological progress

继续开展爱国卫生运动,动员全社会参与

continue launching the patriotic health campaign, mobilizing the whole society to participate in it

建设高素质的卫生工作队伍

build a high-quality contingent of medical personnel

加强医德医风建设

（1）improve the medical ethics and medical style of work

（2）foster fine professional ethics and style of work among medical personnel

加快卫生管理体制改革

accelerate the reform of the management system of public health

发展和完善农村合作医疗制度

develop and improve the system of rural cooperative medical services

推进城镇医疗保障制度的改革

promote the reform of the urban medical security system

发展体育运动，增强人民体质

develop physical culture and sports and improve the people's physical fitness

实施全民健身计划

（1）carry out the physical fitness plan for the entire population

（2）carry out the body-building plan for all Chinese people

实施奥运争光计划

carry out the program of "striving for Olympic glory"

开展群众性体育运动

（1）develop mass sports activities（or mass physical culture）

（2）develop popular sports

提高体育队伍素质和竞技运动水平

improve the quality of sports contingent and raise the level of competitive sports

贯彻群众体育与竞技体育协调发展的方针

carry out the principle of achieving coordinated development between popular sports and competitive sports

树立良好的体育道德和竞技风尚
foster fine sports ethics and sportsmanship

（五）文化环境
Cultural Environment

营造良好的文化环境
create a healthy cultural environment

深入持久地开展群众性精神文明创建活动
conduct mass activities to promote cultural and ideological progress in depth and in a protracted way

促进文化市场健康发展
facilitate the sound development of the markets for cultural products

加强文化基础设施建设
build more cultural establishments

建设好图书馆、博物馆、科技馆、文化馆、革命历史纪念馆等公共设施
do a good job of the construction of libraries, museums, science and technology halls, cultural centers, memorial halls of revolutionary history and other cultural facilities

加强爱国主义教育基地建设
strengthen the building of bases for patriotic education

扩大广播电视覆盖网
extend the network of radio and television broadcast

重视科学、历史、文化的遗产和革命文物的保护
pay attention to the protection of scientific, historical and cultural heritage and revolutionary relics

提倡健康文明的生活方式
advocate healthy and civilized lifestyle (or way of life)

提高群众精神文化生活的质量
improve the cultural life of the masses

开展对外文化交流

conduct cultural exchange with other countries

坚持以我为主、为我所用的原则

uphold the principle of keeping our own culture as the base and making use of that of others

博采各国文化之长

draw on strong points of the cultures of other countries

向世界展示中国文化建设的成就

introduce China's achievements of cultural advancement to the world

坚决抵制各种腐朽思想文化的侵蚀

resolutely resist the corrosion of various decadent ideas and cultures

（六）党的知识分子政策
The Party's Policy Toward Intellectuals

尊重知识，尊重人才

(1) respect knowledge, respect trained personnel

(2) respect for knowledge (or for learning) and for competent people

知识分子是工人阶级的一部分。

Intellectuals are part of the working class.

知识分子在现代化建设中起着重要作用。

Intellectuals are playing an important role in the drive for modernization.

认真贯彻党的知识分子政策

conscientiously implement the Party's policy toward intellectuals

充分发挥知识分子的积极性和创造性

give full play to the initiative and creativity of intellectuals

提倡知识分子又红又专

encourage intellectuals to become both "red and expert" (or both politically conscious and professionally competent)

知识分子要加强学习,提高自己。

Intellectuals should study hard and better themselves.

知识分子要努力成为先进思想的传播者、科学技术的开拓者、"四有"公民的培育者和优秀精神产品的生产者。

Intellectuals should strive to become propagators of advanced thoughts, pioneers in the development of science and technology, educators training people to be citizens with high ideals, moral integrity, a good education and a strong sense of discipline, and producers of excellent intellectual works.

知识分子要同广大工人、农民一起,为中华民族的振兴建功立业。

Intellectuals should contribute hand in hand with workers and peasants to the rejuvenation of the Chinese nation.

九、社会主义精神文明建设
Socialist Cultural and Ideological Progress

(一)精神文明建设的战略地位
The Strategic Position of Cultural and Ideological Progress

社会主义精神文明建设是社会主义社会的重要特征,是现代化建设的重要目标和重要保证。

Socialist cultural and ideological progress is an important characteristic of a socialist society, and serves as an important objective and guarantee for the modernization drive.

我们要建设的社会主义国家,不但要有高度的物质文明,而且要有高度的精神文明。

The socialist country we are going to build should not only have a high degree of material civilization, but also advanced social culture and ideology.

要在经济建设为中心的前提下,使物质文明建设和精神文明建设相互促进,协调发展。

It is imperative to complement and coordinate the development of material progress and cultural and ideological progress under the premise of centering on economic development.

社会主义精神文明建设必须紧紧围绕经济建设这个中心,为经济建设和改革开放提供强大的精神动力和智力支持。

The socialist cultural and ideological progress must be closely linked to the central task of economic development, providing economic development, reform and opening-up with a powerful ideological driving force and strong intellectual support.

任何时候都不能以牺牲精神文明为代价换取经济一时的发展。

(1) At no time should cultural and ideological progress be sacrificed in return for temporary economic development.

(2) We must never seek temporary economic development at the cost of cultural and ideological progress.

(二) 社会主义精神文明建设的指导思想和奋斗目标
Guidelines and Objectives for Promoting Socialist Cultural and Ideological Progress

以马克思列宁主义、毛泽东思想、邓小平理论为指导
take Marxism-Leninism, Mao Zedong Thought and Deng Xiaoping Theory as the guide

坚持党的基本路线、基本纲领和基本方针
adhere to the basic line, basic program and basic principle of the Party

加强思想道德建设
promote ideological and ethical progress

发展教育科学文化
(1) develop education, science and culture
(2) develop education, science and cultural undertakings

以科学的理论武装人
arm people's minds with scientific theory

以正确的舆论引导人
guide people in correct public opinion

以高尚的精神塑造人
mould people with noble spirit

以优秀的作品鼓舞人
inspire people with excellent (literary and artistic) works

培育有理想、有道德、有文化、有纪律的社会主义公民

train and bring up socialist citizens who have high ideals, moral integrity, a good education and a strong sense of discipline

提高全民族的思想道德素质和科学文化素质

improve the ideological and ethical quality and the scientific and cultural quality of the whole nation

团结和动员各族人民把我国建设成为富强、民主、文明的社会主义现代化国家

unite and motivate the people of all nationalities to build China into a socialist and modernized country which is prosperous, strong, democratic and civilized (or culturally advanced)

在全民族牢固树立建设有中国特色社会主义的共同理想

firmly establish the common ideas of building socialism with Chinese characteristics for the whole nation

在全民族牢固树立坚持党的基本路线不动摇的坚定信念

firmly establish an unswerving belief in the Party's basic line for the whole nation

实现以思想道德修养、科学教育水平、民主法制观念为主要内容的公民素质的显著提高

achieve (or bring about) a marked improvement in the quality of citizens which focuses on their ideological and ethical attainments, scientific and educational standards, and their awareness of democracy and legality

实现以积极健康、丰富多彩、服务人民为主要要求的文化生活质量的显著提高

achieve a marked improvement in the quality of cultural life which is required mainly to be positive and healthy, rich and colorful, and to serve the people

实现以社会风气、公共秩序、生活环境为主要标志的城乡文明程度的显著提高

achieve a marked improvement in urban and rural civilizations featuring mainly a good social atmosphere, public order and living environment

在全国范围形成物质文明建设和精神文明建设协调发展的良好局面

achieve the coordinated growth of material civilization and cultural and ideological progress across the country

(三)群众性精神文明创建活动
Mass Activities to Promote
Cultural and Ideological Progress

创建文明家庭、文明单位活动

activities of building up civilized households and civilized units

创建文明城市[文明村镇]活动

activities of building up civilized cities [civilized villages and townships]

军民共建、警民共建文明单位活动

activities of building up civilized units with the joint efforts of the military and the civilians (or of the army and the people) and of the police and the civilians (or of the police and the people)

建设社区文化、村镇文化、企业文化、校园文化

build up a community culture, village and township culture, enterprise culture and campus culture

开展群众性文化、卫生、体育和科学普及活动

carry out mass activities on culture, health, sports and popular science

形成文明、健康、崇尚科学的社会风尚

form civilized, healthy and science-upholding social practice

文化、科技、卫生下乡活动

activities to bring culture, science and technology, and medical and health care to the countryside

创建文明行业活动

cultural and ideological building activities among all trades and professions

在与群众生活关系密切的"窗口行业"创建文明服务示范"窗口"

build exemplary "windows" offering civilized services in "window trades" (or in trades serving as "windows") which are closely related with the well-being of the masses

服务行业的承诺制

system of offering guarantees to consumers in service industry

"讲文明树新风"活动

activities of "stressing civility and fostering new practice"

宣传先进集体和先进人物

publicize the advanced groups and individuals

宣传各个领域的先进典型

publicize the role models emerging in various fields

在全社会形成崇尚先进、学习先进的风气

cultivate an atmosphere in which the whole of society respects and learns from the advanced

(四)坚持两手抓、两手都要硬的方针
Adhering to the Principle of
Doing Two Types of Work at the Same Time,
Attaching Equal Importance to Both

加强和改善党对精神文明建设的领导

strengthen and improve the Party's leadership in promoting cultural and ideological progress

在我国的现代化进程中,必须始终坚持一手抓物质文明,一手抓精神文明。

In the process of China's modernization, we must always work for material progress and at the same time for cultural and ideological progress.

两手抓,两手都要硬
(1) do two types of work at the same time, attaching equal importance to both
(2) grasp two links at the same time and attach equal importance to both
(3) work at two tasks and be steadfast with regard to both

两个文明一起抓,两手都要硬
(1) promote both kinds of progress, attaching equal importance to both
(2) pay equal attention to the two kinds of progress, with neither aspect neglected
(3) place (or put) equal emphasis on material progress and cultural and ideological progress, with neither aspect neglected

宣传舆论阵地必须牢牢掌握在党的手里。
The front of publicity and public opinion must be firmly controlled in the hands of the Party.

思想政治工作在新形势下只能加强,不能削弱。
Under the new situation, ideological and political work can only be strengthened, and cannot be weakened by any means.

抓精神文明建设,必须狠狠地抓,一天也不放松地抓,从具体事件抓起。
To promote cultural and ideological progress, we must redouble our efforts and not relax them for a single day, and we should start by dealing with specific cases of wrongdoing.

要按照政治强、业务精、作风正的要求,造就一支高素质的宣传思想文化教育队伍。
It is necessary to build a high-quality contingent of people working on publicity, ideology, culture or education front in line with the requirements of being qualified politically, professionally competent and having a fine style of work.

搞精神文明,关键是党风建设和领导干部以身作则。

The key to promoting cultural and ideological progress lies in the improvement of the Party's style of work and the exemplary role of leading cadres.

十、国防和军队建设
National Defense and Army Building

加强国防和军队建设,是国家安全和现代化建设的基本保证。

To strengthen national defense and army building is the basic guarantee for our national security and modernization drive.

邓小平新时期军队建设思想是毛泽东军事思想的继承和发展,是我军建设和国防建设的科学指南。

Deng Xiaoping's concept of army building in the new period is the continuation and development of Mao Zedong's thinking on military affairs and the scientific guide to building our army and our national defense.

为把我军建设成为一支强大的现代化正规化革命军队而奋斗

strive to build our army into a powerful, modernized and regularized (or standardized) revolutionary army

要按照政治合格、军事过硬、作风优良、纪律严明、保障有力的总要求,积极推进军队的建设和改革。

In line with the general requirements of being qualified politically and competent militarily and having a fine style of work, strict discipline and adequate logistical support, we should press ahead with the army building and reform.

把人民解放军的革命化、现代化、正规化建设提高到一个新水平

make the People's Liberation Army a more revolutionary, modernized and regularized army

我们的军队必须始终不渝地坚持党的绝对领导。

Our army must consistently uphold the absolute leadership of the Communist Party of China.

在思想上、政治上同党中央保持一致
be in agreement with the Party Central Committee ideologically and politically

一切行动听党中央指挥
obey orders of the Party Central Committee in all actions

我们的军队始终要忠于党，忠于人民，忠于国家，忠于社会主义。
Our army should always be loyal to our Party, to the people, to our country and to socialism.

坚持人民军队的性质和宗旨
stick to the nature and purpose of the people's army

贯彻积极防御的军事战略方针
carry out the military strategy of active defense

加强军队的质量建设
improve the quality of the army

走有中国特色的精兵之路
(1) take the road of fewer but better troops with Chinese characteristics
(2) take the road appropriate to China toward fewer but better troops
(3) streamline the army the Chinese way

从严治军
(1) The army should be strict with itself.
(2) be strict with the army

政治工作是我军的生命线。
Political work is the life-blood of our army.

加强军队的思想政治建设
strengthen ideological and political work in the army

发扬我军的优良传统

carry forward the fine traditions of our army

坚定正确的政治方向
firm and correct political orientation

艰苦朴素的工作作风
style of hard work and plain living

灵活机动的战略战术
flexible strategy and tactics

军队在精神文明建设方面要走在全社会前列。
The army should take the lead in the whole society in promoting cultural and ideological progress.

军队要加强教育训练。
The army should intensify its education and training.

全面提高部队的思想政治素质、军事技术素质、科学文化素质
improve in an all-round way the troops' ideological and political quality, military and technological quality, and scientific and cultural quality

提高军队在现代技术特别是高技术条件下的防卫作战能力
upgrade (or improve) the army's defense capabilities (and combat effectiveness) under modern technology and especially high-tech conditions

科技强军
strengthen the army by relying on science and technology

加强国防科技研究
(1) put more efforts in the research in defense-related science and technology
(2) strengthen scientific and technological research for national defense

积极进行国防工业的调整和改革
take effective measures to readjust and reform defense industry (or industries)

逐步更新武器装备
gradually upgrade weapons and other equipment

军队要服从和服务于国家经济建设大局。
(1) The army should subordinate itself to and serve the overall interests of national economic development.
(2) The army should be subordinated to and serve general interest of economic development of our country.

勤俭建军
build the army through diligence and thrift (or through thrift and hard work)

积极支持和参加国家经济建设
actively support and participate in the economic development of the country

培养军地两用人才
train personnel (competent) for both military and civilian services (or jobs)

各级党组织、政府和人民群众要关心、支持国防和军队建设。
Party organizations and governments at all levels and the masses should be concerned about and support the development of national defense and army building.

加强国防教育
intensify defense education

增强全民国防观念
increase the (whole) people's awareness of the importance of national defense

拥政爱民
support the government and cherish the people

拥军优属
support the army and give preferential treatment to families of armymen (or servicemen) and martyrs

巩固军政、军民团结

(1) consolidate the unity between the army and the government and between the army and the people

(2) consolidate the unity of the army and the government and the unity of the army and the civilians

加强民兵预备役部队建设

strengthen the work with regard to the militia and the reserves

完善国防动员体制

improve the mobilization system for national defense

加强中国人民武装警察部队和公安、国家安全部门的建设

strengthen the Chinese People's Armed Police (Force) and the public and state security departments

十一、坚持四项基本原则
Upholding the Four Cardinal Principles

四项基本原则是立国之本。

The Four Cardinal Principles are the foundation of our country.

四项基本原则是改革开放和现代化建设健康发展的保证。

The Four Cardinal Principles guarantee the sound development of the reform, opening up and the drive for modernization.

四项基本原则从改革开放和现代化建设获得新的时代内容。

The Four Cardinal Principles are enriched with contemporary content by the reform, opening up and the drive for modernization.

坚持四项基本原则,必须反对资产阶级自由化。

To adhere to the Four Cardinal Principles, we must combat bourgeois liberalization.

坚持社会主义道路
keep to the socialist road

只有社会主义才能救中国。
(1) Only socialism can save China.
(2) Socialism and socialism alone can save China.

只有社会主义才能发展中国。
(1) Only socialism can develop China.
(2) Socialism and socialism alone can develop China.

社会主义制度是中华人民共和国的根本制度。

The socialist system is the basic system of the People's Republic of China.

要搞清楚什么是社会主义,怎样建设社会主义。

We must be clear about what socialism is and how to build it.

沿着建设有中国特色的社会主义道路前进

advance along the road of building socialism with Chinese characteristics

坚持社会主义,防止和平演变

adhere to socialism and prevent peaceful evolution toward capitalism

社会主义经过一个长过程发展后必然代替资本主义。

After going through a long process of its development, socialism will necessarily supersede capitalism.

坚持人民民主专政

uphold the people's democratic dictatorship

中华人民共和国是工人阶级领导的工农联盟为基础的人民民主专政的社会主义国家。

The People's Republic of China is a socialist state under the people's democratic dictatorship led by the working class and based on the alliance of workers and peasants.

对人民实行民主,对敌人实行专政

practice democracy for the people and enforce dictatorship over the enemy

人民民主专政的国家政权是我们事业健康发展的政治保证。

The state power of the people's democratic dictatorship constitutes the political guarantee for the sound development of our cause.

运用人民民主专政的力量来巩固人民的政权

consolidate the people's power by employing the force of

the people's democratic dictatorship

坚持中国共产党的领导
uphold the leadership of (or by) the Communist Party of China

中国共产党是中国工人阶级的先锋队。
The Communist Party of China is the vanguard of the Chinese working class.

中国共产党是中国各族人民利益的忠实代表。
The Communist Party of China is the faithful representative of the interests of the people of all nationalities in China.

中国共产党是中国社会主义事业的领导核心。
(1) The Communist Party of China is the force at the core leading China's cause of socialism (forward).
(2) The Communist Party of China is the leading core (or the core of the leadership) for (or in) China's socialist cause.

中国共产党是领导建设有中国特色社会主义事业的核心力量。
The Communist Party of China is the force at the core leading the cause of building socialism with Chinese characteristics.

没有中国共产党就不会有现代化的社会主义中国。
Without the Chinese Communist Party, there would be no modernized socialist China.

坚持马克思列宁主义、毛泽东思想
uphold Marxism-Leninism and Mao Zedong Thought

把马克思主义的普遍真理同我国的具体实际结合起来，走自己的道路，建设有中国特色的社会主义。
We must integrate the universal truth of Marxism with the concrete realities of China, blaze a path of our own (or take our own road) and build a socialism with Chinese characteristics.

马克思列宁主义、毛泽东思想一定不能丢，丢了就丧失根本。

We must never discard Marxism-Leninism and Mao Zedong Thought. If we did, we would lose our foundation.

一定要以我国改革开放和现代化建设的实际问题、以我们正在做的事情为中心,着眼于马克思主义理论的运用,着眼于对实际问题的理论思考,着眼于新的实践和新的发展。

Centering on the practical problems in the reform, opening up and the modernization drive and on things we are doing, we must emphasize the application of Marxist theory, the theoretical study of practical problems, and new practice and new development.

在当代中国,坚持邓小平理论,就是真正坚持马克思列宁主义、毛泽东思想。

In present-day China, adhering to Deng Xiaoping Theory means genuinely adhering to Marxism-Leninism and Mao Zedong Thought.

在重大问题上要旗帜鲜明,分清是非界限。

(1) We should distinguish right from wrong on major issues with a clear-cut stand.

(2) We should draw (or make) a distinction between right and wrong on major issues with a clear-cut stand.

分清社会主义公有制为主体、多种所有制经济共同发展同私有化的界限

distinguish common development of various types of ownership with socialist public ownership in the dominant position from privatization

分清社会主义民主同西方议会民主的界限

distinguish socialist democracy from parliamentary democracy practiced in Western countries

分清辩证唯物主义、历史唯物主义同唯心主义、形而上学的界限

distinguish dialectical materialism and historical materialism from idealism and metaphysics

分清社会主义思想文化同封建主义、资本主义腐朽

思想文化的界限

distinguish socialist ideology and culture from decadent feudal and capitalist ideologies and cultures

分清学习西方先进东西同崇洋媚外的界限

distinguish studying advanced things of the West from worshipping foreign things and toadying to foreign powers

分清文明健康生活方式同消极颓废生活方式的界限

distinguish civilized and healthy lifestyle from dispirited and decadent lifestyle

十二、祖国统一大业
The Great Cause of Reunification of the Motherland

推进祖国和平统一

promote the peaceful reunification of the motherland

邓小平"一国两制"的科学构想

Deng Xiaoping's scientific concept of "one country, two systems"

"一国两制"构想的基本内容是在祖国统一的前提下,国家的主体坚持社会主义制度,同时在台湾、香港、澳门保持原有的资本主义制度和生活方式长期不变。

The basic idea of the concept of "one country, two systems" is that on the premise of reunification of the motherland, the main part (or the main body) of China (or of the nation, or of the country) will stick to the socialist system while Taiwan, Hong Kong and Macao will retain the previous (or current) capitalist system and way of life (or lifestyle) for a long time to come.

"一国两制"构想是推进祖国和平统一大业的基本方针。

The concept of "one country, two systems" is the basic principle for promoting the great cause of the peaceful reunification of the motherland.

中国对香港恢复行使主权

China's resumption of the exercise of sovereignty over Hong Kong

香港回归祖国

Hong Kong's return to the motherland

坚定不移地贯彻执行"一国两制"、"港人治港"、高度自治的方针

unswervingly implement the policies of "one country, two systems", "Hong Kong people administering Hong Kong" and a high degree of autonomy

《中华人民共和国香港特别行政区基本法》

The Basic Law of the Hong Kong Special Administrative Region of the People's Republic of China

香港特别行政区是中华人民共和国不可分离的部分。

The Hong Kong Special Administrative Region (HKSAR) is an inalienable part of the People's Republic of China.

在国家主体坚持实行社会主义制度的条件下,香港继续实行资本主义制度,保持原有的社会、经济制度不变,生活方式不变,法律基本不变。

Hong Kong will continue to practice the capitalist system, with its previous socio-economic system and way of life remaining unchanged and its laws basically unchanged, while the main part of the nation persists in the socialist system.

保持香港原有的资本主义制度和生活方式,五十年不变

keep Hong Kong's previous capitalist system and way of life unchanged for 50 years

香港特别行政区享有基本法赋予的高度自治权,包括行政管理权、立法权、独立的司法权和终审权。

The HKSAR enjoys a high degree of autonomy as provided for by the Basic Law, which embodies the executive, legislative and independent judicial power, including that of final adjudication.

中央人民政府负责管理与香港特别行政区有关的外交事务,负责管理香港特别行政区的防务。

The Central People's Government is responsible for the foreign affairs relating to the HKSAR and for the defense of the

HKSAR.

中国人民解放军驻香港部队担负香港特别行政区的防务。

The Chinese People's Liberation Army Hong Kong Garrison takes on the defense of the HKSAR.

香港将继续保持其自由港的地位和国际金融、贸易、航运中心的地位。

Hong Kong will retain the status of free port and an international financial, trade and shipping center.

保持香港长期繁荣稳定

maintain long-term prosperity and stability of Hong Kong

香港将根据基本法的规定循序渐进地发展民主。

Hong Kong will develop democracy gradually in accordance with the Basic Law.

香港特别行政区行政长官依照基本法的规定对中央人民政府和香港特别行政区负责。

The Chief Executive of the HKSAR is accountable to the Central People's Government and the HKSAR in accordance with the provisions of the Basic Law.

中国对澳门恢复行使主权

China's resumption of the exercise of sovereignty over Macao

《中华人民共和国澳门特别行政区基本法》

The Basic Law of the Macao Special Administrative Region of the People's Republic of China

台湾是中国神圣领土不可分割的一部分。

Taiwan is an inalienable (or integral) part of the sacred territory of China.

"和平统一、一国两制"是中国政府解决台湾问题的基本方针。

The basic principle of the Chinese government for settling the Taiwan issue is that of "peaceful reunification and one country, two systems".

世界上只有一个中国。

There is but (or only) one China in the world.

中华人民共和国政府是代表全中国的唯一合法政府。

The government of the People's Republic of China is the sole legal government representing the whole of China.

坚持一个中国的原则

(1) stick to the principle of one China

(2) stick to the one-China principle

(3) stick to the principle that there is but (or only) one China

反对分裂，反对"台独"，反对制造"两个中国"、"一中一台"

oppose splitting, the "independence of Taiwan" and the attempt to create "two Chinas" or "one China, one Taiwan"

反对外国势力干涉中国统一

oppose any interference in China's reunification by foreign forces

绝不允许任何势力以任何方式改变台湾是中国一部分的地位。

We shall never allow any forces whatsoever to change Taiwan's status as part of China in any way.

要努力实现和平统一，但不能承诺放弃使用武力。

We shall strive to realize peaceful reunification, but we shall not undertake to renounce the use of force.

发展两岸关系，推进祖国和平统一进程

develop relations between the two sides (of the Taiwan Straits) and promote the peaceful reunification of the motherland

大力发展两岸经济、科技、文化等领域的交流与合作

spare no efforts in expanding exchanges and cooperation **between the two sides in economic, scientific, technological and cultural areas (or in various fields such as economy, sci-**

ence, technology and culture)

加速实现两岸直接通邮、通航、通商
speed up the establishment of direct links of (or for) postal, air and shipping services and trade between the two sides

加强两岸人员往来
promote mutual visits of people between the two sides

我们寄希望于具有光荣传统的台湾同胞。
We place our hopes on our compatriots in Taiwan who are endowed with the glorious tradition of patriotism.

中国共产党和中国政府郑重呼吁在一个中国的原则下两岸进行政治谈判。
The Communist Party of China and the Chinese government solemnly appeal that the two sides conduct political negotiations under the principle of one China.

祖国的完全统一和民族的全面振兴一定能够实现。
The complete reunification of the motherland and the all-round rejuvenation of the Chinese nation can certainly be achieved.

十三、国际形势和对外政策
The International Situation and Our Foreign Policy

（一）国际形势
The International Situation

当今世界正处在大变动的历史时期。

The world today is in a historical period of great change (or of momentous transition).

当前国际形势总体上继续趋向缓和。

At present, the international situation as a whole is becoming more relaxed.

和平与发展是当今时代的主题。

Peace and development are the main themes of the present era.

多极化趋势日益明显。

The trend toward multi-polarity (or trend of multi-polarization) is becoming increasingly clear.

经济、科技全球化趋势加速发展。

(1) The development of globalization trends in economy, science and technology are speeded up.

(2) The trends of economic globalization and scientific and technological globalization develop more rapidly.

世界上各种力量出现新的分化和组合。

World forces are experiencing a new split and realignment.

大国之间的关系经历着重大而又深刻的调整。

Relations between the big countries (or big powers) are undergoing major and profound adjustments.

各种区域性、洲际性的合作组织空前活跃。

Regional and intercontinental organizations of cooperation are active as never before.

广大发展中国家的总体实力在增强。

The overall strength of the great number of developing countries is growing.

各国人民要求平等相待、友好相处的呼声日益高涨。

The call of the people of all countries for treating each other on an equal footing and living together in amity is becoming louder and louder.

要和平、求合作、促发展已经成为时代的主流。

It has become the mainstream of the times to desire peace, seek cooperation and promote development.

在相当长的时期内，避免新的世界大战是可能的，争取一个良好的国际和平环境和周边环境是可以实现的。

For a fairly long period of time to come, it will be possible to avert a new world war and secure a favorable, peaceful international environment and maintain good relations with the surrounding countries.

冷战思维依然存在。

The Cold War mentality still exists.

霸权主义和强权政治仍然是威胁世界和平与稳定的主要根源。

Hegemonism and power politics continue to be the main source of threat to world peace and stability.

不公正、不合理的国际经济旧秩序还在损害着发展中国家的利益。

The unjust and irrational old international economic order is still infringing upon the interests of developing countries.

贫富差距在扩大。

The gap in wealth is widening.

利用"人权"等问题干涉他国内政的现象还很严重。

It is still serious that human rights and other issues are used to interfere in the internal affairs of other countries.

因民族、宗教、领土等因素而引发的局部冲突时起时伏。

Local conflicts due to ethnic, religious and territorial factors crop up from time to time.

世界仍不安宁。

The world is not yet tranquil.

(二)独立自主的和平外交政策
Independent Foreign Policy of Peace

坚持邓小平的外交思想

adhere to the ideas of Deng Xiaoping about diplomatic work

始终不渝地奉行独立自主的和平外交政策

consistently pursue an independent foreign policy of peace

维护我国的独立和主权

safeguard our country's independence and sovereignty

促进世界的和平与发展

promote world peace and development

促进人类进步事业

promote the cause of human progress

对于一切国际事务,我们都要从中国人民和世界人民的根本利益出发,根据事情本身的是非曲直,决定自己的立场和政策。

In international affairs, we should determine our position and policies by proceeding from the fundamental interests of the people of China and other countries and judging each case on its own merits.

在处理国际事务中,中国严格遵守联合国宪章和公认的国际关系准则,坚持实事求是和伸张正义的原则立场。

In handling international affairs, China abides strictly by the United Nations Charter and the acknowledged norms of international relations and adheres to the principled position of seeking truth from facts and upholding justice.

中国不屈从于任何外来压力,不同任何大国或国家集团结盟,不搞军事集团,不参加军备竞赛,不进行军事扩张。

China will not yield to any outside pressure or enter into alliance with any big power or group of countries, nor will China establish any military bloc, join in the arms race or seek military expansion.

反对霸权主义,维护世界和平
oppose hegemonism and safeguard world peace

国与国之间应通过协商和平解决彼此的纠纷和争端,不应诉诸武力或以武力相威胁。

All countries should settle their disputes and conflicts through peaceful consultations instead of resorting to force or the threat of it.

任何国家都不能以任何借口干涉他国内政,更不能恃强凌弱,侵略、欺负和颠覆别的国家。

No country should interfere in the internal affairs of another country under any pretext, still less use its strength to humiliate the weak, invade, bully or subvert other countries.

我们不把自己的社会制度和意识形态强加于人,也决不允许别国把他们的社会制度和意识形态强加于我们。

We do not impose our social system and ideology upon others, nor will we allow other countries to impose theirs upon us.

中国反对利用人权问题干涉别国内政。

(1) China is opposed to the use of the issue of human rights to interfere in other countries' internal affairs.

(2) China is opposed to any attempt to interfere in a country's internal affairs on the pretext of human rights.

(3) China opposes one country using the human rights issue to interfere in the internal affairs of another country.

坚持和平共处五项原则

adhere to the Five Principles of Peaceful Coexistence (i.e. mutual respect for sovereignty and territorial integrity, mutual non-aggression, non-interference in each other's internal affairs, equality and mutual benefit, and peaceful coexistence)

要致力于推动建立公正合理的国际政治经济新秩序。

We shall work for promoting the establishment of a just and rational new international political and economic order.

我们主张在和平共处五项原则的基础上建立国际新秩序。

We advocate the establishment of a new international order on the basis of the Five Principles of Peaceful Coexistence.

要尊重世界的多样性。

It is necessary to respect the diversity of the world.

各国都有权选择符合本国国情的社会制度、发展战略和生活方式。

All countries are entitled to choose the social systems, development strategies and lifestyles that suit their own conditions.

各国的事情要由各国人民自己作主。

The affairs of a country should be decided upon by its own people.

国际上的事情要由大家商量解决。

Global issues should be dealt with through consultations by all countries.

要坚持睦邻友好。

(1) The good-neighborly policy should be upheld.

(2) We should keep good relations with neighboring countries.

进一步发展同周边国家的睦邻友好关系

further develop our friendly and good-neighborly relations with the countries bordering China

进一步加强同第三世界国家的团结和合作

further strengthen our solidarity and cooperation with the Third World countries

中国永远属于第三世界。

China shall always belong to the Third World.

中国将一如既往,同广大发展中国家相互支持,密切配合,共同维护正当权益。

China will, as always, join the vast number of developing countries in mutual support and close cooperation to safeguard our lawful rights and interests.

要在和平共处五项原则的基础上,继续改善和发展同发达国家的关系。

We should further improve and develop our relations with developed countries on the basis of the Five Principles of Peaceful Coexistence.

国与国之间应超越社会制度和意识形态的差异,相互尊重,友好相处。

All countries should respect each other and live together in amity regardless of differences in their social systems and ideologies.

要寻求共同利益的汇合点,扩大互利合作,共同对付人类生存和发展所面临的挑战。

All countries should seek the point where their common interests converge, expand mutually beneficial cooperation and work together to take up the challenge facing mankind for survival and development.

对国与国之间的分歧要坚持对话,不搞对抗,妥善加以解决。

It is necessary to persist in dialogue, not confrontation, properly handling the differences between various countries.

求同存异,发展合作

(1) seek common ground while reserving differences and increase cooperation

(2) seek common ground while putting aside disagreements and enhance cooperation

反对动辄进行制裁或以制裁相威胁

be opposed to imposing or threatening to impose sanctions without good reason

要坚持平等互利的原则,同世界各国和地区广泛开展贸易往来、经济技术合作和科学文化交流,促进共同发展。

Pursuant to the principle of equality and mutual benefit, we should conduct extensive trade, economic and technological cooperation and scientific and cultural exchanges with all countries and regions to promote common development.

要积极参与多边外交活动。

We should take an active part in multilateral diplomatic activities.

充分发挥我国在联合国以及其他国际组织中的作用

give full play to China's role in the United Nations and other international organizations

中国共产党要坚持在独立自主、完全平等、互相尊重、互不干涉内部事务原则的基础上,同一切愿与中国共产党交往的各国政党发展新型的党际关系,促进国家关系的发展。

On the basis of the principles of independence, complete equality, mutual respect and non-interference in each other's internal affairs, the Communist Party of China will continue to develop new type of inter-party relations with all political parties of various countries which are ready to have contacts with the Communist Party of China with a view to promoting state relations.

中国是维护世界和平和地区稳定的坚定力量。

China is a staunch force for safeguarding world peace and regional stability.

中国进行社会主义现代化建设,需要一个长期的和平国际环境特别是良好的周边环境。

In carrying out the socialist modernization program, China needs a long-term peaceful international environment, and above all, China needs to maintain good relations with the surrounding countries.

中国的发展不会对任何国家构成威胁。

China's development will not pose a threat to any other country.

中国主张根据公正、合理、全面、均衡的原则实行有效的裁军和军控。

China stands for effective disarmament and arms control carried out in a principle of fairness, rationality, comprehensiveness and balance.

中国一向主张全面禁止和彻底销毁核武器。

China always stands for the complete prohibition and thorough destruction of nuclear weapons.

中国永远不称霸。

China will never seek hegemony.

中国人民愿意同世界各国人民一道,为促进和平与发展的崇高事业,为开创人类更加美好的未来,作出不懈的努力。

The Chinese people are ready to join hands with the people of other countries in making unremitting efforts to promote the lofty cause of peace and development and work for a brighter future for mankind.

十四、面向新世纪的中国共产党
The Communist Party of China Facing the New Century

(一)党的建设新的伟大工程
A New Great Project of Party Building

中国共产党是全国各族人民的领导核心。

The Communist Party of China is the leading core of the people of all nationalities in China.

我们全部事业的成败,关键在党。

The key to the success of our entire cause lies in the Party.

要坚持、加强和改善党的领导。

It is essential to uphold, strengthen and improve the leadership of the Party.

继续推进党的建设新的伟大工程

continue to advance the new great project of Party building

要把党建设成为用邓小平理论武装起来、全心全意为人民服务、思想上政治上组织上完全巩固、能够经受住各种风险、始终走在时代前列、领导全国人民建设有中国特色社会主义的马克思主义政党。

It is essential to make the Party a Marxist political party that is armed with Deng Xiaoping Theory, that serves the people wholeheartedly, that is fully consolidated ideologically, politically and organizationally, that can withstand all kinds of risks (or all trials and tribulations), that always advances in the forefront of the times and leads the people of the whole country in building socialism with Chinese characteristics.

从思想上、组织上、作风上全面加强党的建设
strengthen Party building in an all-round way — in ideology, organization and style of work

坚持党的工人阶级先锋队的性质
maintain the nature of the Party as the vanguard of the working class

不断提高党的领导水平和执政水平
(1) always try to improve the Party's leading and governing ability
(2) constantly make the Party exercise more effective leadership and power

不断增强拒腐防变的能力
(1) always try to guard against corruption and degeneration
(2) constantly enhance the ability to resist corruption and guard against deterioration

继承党的优良传统
carry forward the Party's fine traditions

坚持和维护党的团结和统一
uphold and safeguard the unity and unification of the Party

增强党的凝聚力和战斗力
enhance the Party's cohesiveness and fighting capacity

(二)党的思想建设
Party Building in Ideology

加强党的思想建设,根本的是坚定不移地用邓小平理论武装全党,充分发挥党的思想政治优势。

To strengthen Party building ideologically, it is essential to unswervingly arm the entire Party with Deng Xiaoping Theory and give full play to the ideological and political strength of the Party.

全党要重视学习,善于学习,兴起一个学习马列主

义、毛泽东思想特别是邓小平理论的新高潮。

The entire Party should attach great importance to study, be adept at studying and usher in a new upsurge in studying Marxism-Leninism, Mao Zedong Thought and particularly Deng Xiaoping Theory.

全党要深入学习邓小平理论。

The entire Party should study Deng Xiaoping Theory in depth.

各级领导干部首先要带头学好邓小平理论。

Leading cadres at all levels should take the lead in studying Deng Xiaoping Theory.

完整、准确地把握邓小平理论的科学体系

comprehensively and accurately master the scientific system of Deng Xiaoping Theory

领会邓小平理论的基本观点和基本精神

grasp (or understand) the basic ideas (or viewpoints) and the essence of Deng Xiaoping Theory

从各自工作领域对邓小平理论的有关内容进行系统钻研和理解

systematically analyze (or dig into) and understand the relevant aspects of Deng Xiaoping Theory in terms of the respective fields of work

在县级以上领导干部中进行以讲学习、讲政治、讲正气为主要内容的党性党风教育

educate the cadres at and above the county level in Party spirit and conduct, focusing mainly on the need to study, to be politically minded and to be honest and upright

在全党造成认真学习的风气，民主讨论的风气，积极探索的风气，求真务实的风气

(1) make it a common practice within the entire Party to study conscientiously, hold democratic discussions, try to explore new ways and be realistic and pragmatic

(2) strive to create in the whole Party an atmosphere of serious study, democratic discussion, enthusiastic exploration,

seeking truth and dealing with concrete matters

弘扬理论联系实际的马克思主义学风
carry forward the Marxist style of study of integrating theory with practice (or linking theory and practice)

坚持解放思想、实事求是的思想路线
adhere to the ideological line of emancipating the mind and seeking truth from facts

坚持理论联系实际,学以致用
continue to integrate theory with practice and study for the sake of application

提高马克思主义理论水平,提高解决实际问题的能力
acquire a better understanding of the theory of Marxism, learn to better solve practical problems

在改造客观世界的同时改造主观世界
transform our subjective world while transforming the objective world

身体力行共产主义思想和共产主义道德
earnestly put into practice the communist ideology and communist morality (or ethics)

增强贯彻执行党的基本理论、基本路线、基本纲领的自觉性和坚定性
increase the consciousness and staunchness in carrying out the Party's basic theory, basic line and basic program

拿起批评和自我批评的武器,开展积极的思想斗争
take up the weapon of criticism and self-criticism to wage active ideological struggle

(三)党的组织建设
The Party's Organizational Building

加强党的组织建设,根本的是把党建设成坚强的领导核心,充分发挥党的组织优势。

To strengthen Party building organizationally, it is essential to make the Party the strong leading core and give full play to its organizational strength.

完善和发展民主集中制
improve and develop democratic centralism

进一步发扬党内民主
further enhance inner-Party democracy

保障党员的民主权利
guarantee the democratic rights of Party members

疏通和拓宽党内民主渠道
clear and widen channels for inner-Party democracy

充分发挥全党的积极性和创造性
give full play to the initiative and creativity of the whole Party

党员个人服从党的组织，少数服从多数，下级组织服从上级组织，全党各个组织和全体党员服从党的全国代表大会和中央委员会。
Individual Party members are subordinate to the Party organization, the minority is subordinate to the majority, the lower Party organizations are subordinate to the higher Party organizations, and all the constituent organizations and members of the Party are subordinate to the National Congress and the Central Committee of the Party.

要维护中央权威，在思想上、政治上同中央保持一致。
We should safeguard the authority of the Central Committee of the Party and be in agreement with it on ideological and political matters (or be in agreement with it ideologically and politically).

保证党的路线和中央的决策顺利贯彻执行
ensure the smooth implementation of the Party's line and the Central Committee's policy decisions

完善党的代表大会制度

improve the system of Party congresses

健全各级党委集体领导和个人分工负责相结合的制度

(1) improve the system whereby the collective leadership by Party committees at all levels is combined with division of work and individual responsibility

(2) improve the system of combining collective leadership by Party committees at all levels and division of labor with individual responsibility

发挥地方党委在同级各种组织中的领导核心作用

ensure that local Party committees play the leading core role in the various organizations at corresponding levels

领导干部要带头遵守民主集中制的各项规定,维护大局,严守纪律。

Leading cadres should take the lead in observing the various rules of democratic centralism, protecting the interests of the Party as a whole and strictly observing discipline.

贯彻执行干部队伍革命化、年轻化、知识化、专业化方针

implement the principle of making the contingent of cadres more revolutionary, younger, better educated and more competent professionally

建设一支适应社会主义现代化建设需要的高素质干部队伍

foster a contingent of highly qualified cadres who can meet the requirements of the socialist modernization drive

把各级领导班子建设成为坚决贯彻党的基本理论和基本路线、全心全意为人民服务、具有领导现代化建设能力、团结坚强的领导集体

turn the leading bodies at all levels into united, staunch collective leaderships that resolutely carry out the Party's basic theory and basic line, serve the people wholeheartedly and are capable of leading the modernization drive

提高领导干部的政治业务素质

improve the political and professional quality of the leading cadres

领导干部一定要讲政治。
The leading cadres must give heed to politics.

讲学习、讲政治、讲正气
（1）emphasize the need to study, to be politically minded and to be honest and upright
（2）give heed to (or pay heed to) study, politics and healthy tendencies (or trends)
（3）stress study, politics and healthy tendencies

领导干部要重视学习,加强学习,不断提高理论修养和知识水平。
The leading cadres should pay attention to and make greater efforts at study, constantly improving their understanding of (Marxist) theory and raising their level of knowledge.

学理论,学历史,学经济,学科技,学管理,学法律
study (Marxist) theory, history, economics, science and technology, management and law

学习一切需要学习的东西
（1）study everything we need to study
（2）study everything needed to be learned

党的高级干部要具有社会主义政治家的素质。
The Party's senior cadres should be qualified socialist statesmen.

严重的问题在于教育干部。
The serious problem is the education of the cadres.

加强干部教育培训工作
strengthen the education and training of (or for) the cadres

加快干部制度改革步伐
accelerate the reform of the cadre(s) system

干部管理工作要扩大民主,完善考核,推进交流,加

强监督。

In managing affairs relating to cadres, it is necessary to enhance democracy, improve their assessment, promote their exchanges and tighten supervision over them.

使优秀人才脱颖而出

enable competent people (or talented persons) to emerge (or to reveal themselves)

要使干部能上能下

see that our cadres are ready to go up and equally ready to come down (or ready to take a lower as well as a higher post)

选拔干部必须全面贯彻德才兼备的原则。

In selecting cadres, it is imperative to thoroughly carry out the principle of having both ability and political integrity (or both political integrity and professional competence).

坚持任人唯贤,反对任人唯亲

persist in appointing people on their merits and oppose favoritism

要把群众公认是坚决执行党的路线、实绩突出、清正廉洁的干部及时选拔到领导岗位上来。

It is imperative to promptly promote to leading posts those cadres who are generally acknowledged as having firmly carried out the Party's line and scored outstanding achievements and being honest and clean.

培养和选拔大批能够担当重任的优秀年轻干部

train (or foster) and select a large number of excellent young cadres who can shoulder important tasks

培养和选拔妇女干部、少数民族干部和非党干部

train (or foster) and select women cadres, cadres from among ethnic minorities (or minority nationality cadres) and non-Party cadres

完善干部(离)退休制度

improve the cadre retirement system

从政治上关心、生活上照顾老干部,发挥老干部的作

用

take good care of veteran cadres politically and in terms of the well-being, encouraging them to play their role

党的基层组织是党的全部工作和战斗力的基础。

The grassroots Party organizations (or primary organizations of the Party, or primary Party organizations) are the locus of all the Party's work and the base of its fighting capacity.

加强和改进党的基层组织建设,要围绕党的基本路线,为党的中心任务服务。

The work of consolidating and improving grassroots Party organizations should be geared to the Party's basic line and serve its central task.

党的基层组织要用改革精神研究新情况新问题,改进工作方法、工作作风和活动方式。

Grassroots Party organizations should study new situations and problems in a spirit of reform and improve their methods and style of work and their ways of conducting activities.

党的基层组织要认真做好对党员的教育、管理和监督,增强解决自身矛盾的能力。

Grassroots Party organizations should conscientiously educate, manage and supervise Party members and enhance the ability to solve their own problems.

党的基层组织都要从各自的特点出发,认真履行党章规定的职责。

In light of their own characteristics, all grassroots Party organizations should earnestly perform their duties prescribed by the Constitution of the Party.

努力把党的基层组织建设成为贯彻党的路线方针政策、团结和带领群众完成本单位任务的坚强战斗堡垒。

Strive to turn grassroots Party organizations into a staunch, powerful force (or into staunch fighting bastions) that can carry out the Party's line, principles and policies, and unite with the masses and lead them in fulfilling the tasks of their own units.

农村要进一步搞好以党支部为核心的村级组织建设。

In rural areas, it is necessary to make a greater success of building village-level organizations with Party branches as the nuclei.

国有企业要充分发挥党组织的政治核心作用。

In state-owned enterprises, it is necessary to give full play to the role of Party organizations as political nuclei.

（四）党的作风建设
Improving the Party's Style of Work

加强党的作风建设，根本的是坚持全心全意为人民服务的宗旨，充分发挥党密切联系群众的优势。

To improve the Party's style of work, it is essential to stick to the aim (or purpose) of serving the people wholeheartedly and give full play to the Party's strength in forging close links with the masses.

执政党的党风关系党的生死存亡。

(1) A fine style of work is vital to the very existence of the party in power.

(2) The style of work of a political party in power is a matter that determines its very existence.

(3) The work style of a party in power is a matter of life and death for this party.

端正党风是端正社会风气的关键。

Improving Party conduct (or Party work style) is the key to improving general social conduct.

发扬党的三大作风
carry forward the Party's three important styles of work

理论和实践相结合的作风
style of integrating theory with practice

和人民群众紧密地联系在一起的作风

style of forging close links with the masses

批评和自我批评的作风
style of practicing criticism and self-criticism

共产党员要倾听群众呼声,关心群众疾苦,为群众办实事、办好事。

Party members (or members of the Communist Party, or Communists) should listen attentively to the voice of the masses, help alleviate their hardships (or be concerned about their weal and woe) and do practical things in their interests.

党的干部必须正确行使人民赋予的权力,决不能以权谋私。

Party cadres must correctly exercise the power entrusted to them by the people and must never abuse power for personal gain.

党的干部必须把对上负责和对群众负责统一起来,决不能把二者割裂开来、对立起来。

Party cadres must combine responsibility to their superiors with responsibility to the masses, never separating the two or setting them against each other.

党的干部必须在工作中坚持群众路线,深入实际调查研究,决不能搞官僚主义、形式主义、强迫命令。

In their work, Party cadres must uphold the mass line, go deep into the realities for investigation and study, and never indulge in bureaucracy, formalism or coercion.

一切为了群众,一切相信群众,一切依靠群众

(1) serve the interests of the masses, and have faith in and rely on the masses in everything we do

(2) everything for the masses, faith in and reliance on the masses in everything

(五)反对腐败
The Fight Against Corruption

反对腐败是关系党和国家生死存亡的严重政治斗

争。

The fight against corruption is a grave political struggle vital to the very existence of the Party and the state.

在整个改革开放过程中都要反对腐败,警钟长鸣。

We should fight (or combat) corruption and continuously give the warning throughout the process of reform and opening to the outside world.

反对腐败既要树立持久作战的思想,又要一个一个地打好阶段性战役。

We should be mentally prepared to fight a protracted war against corruption, and we should win battles one by one and stage by stage.

抓好领导干部廉洁自律

make sure that leading cadres are clear, honest and self-disciplined

查处大案要案

investigate and deal with major cases

纠正部门和行业不正之风

rectify unsound practices (or correct unhealthy tendencies) in departments and trades

各级党委务必做到旗帜鲜明,态度坚定,抓反腐败工作锲而不舍。

Party committees at all levels must take a clear-cut stand, have a staunch manner and firmly persevere in the work for fighting corruption.

要标本兼治,防范和消除腐败。

We should seek both temporary and permanent solutions so as to prevent and eliminate corruption.

教育是基础,法制是保证,监督是关键。

Education is the basis, the legal system is the guarantee, and supervision is the key.

通过深化改革,不断铲除腐败现象滋生蔓延的土壤。

By deepening the reform, we should gradually eradicate

the soil for the breeding and spreading of corruption.

党委统一领导，党政齐抓共管，纪委组织协调，部门各负其责，依靠群众的支持和参与，坚决遏制腐败现象。

With Party committees exercising unified leadership, Party and government organs exerting concerted efforts, discipline inspection commissions organizing and coordinating the work and departments assuming their respective responsibilities, and relying on the support and participation of the masses, we shall resolutely check corruption.

加强勤政廉政建设

(1) make greater efforts to keep government functionaries honest and industrious

(2) make greater efforts to build an honest, clean and industrious government

(3) step up the building of an honest (or a clean) and industrious government

领导干部要以身作则，模范地遵纪守法，自觉接受监督，抵制腐朽思想的侵蚀，作艰苦奋斗、廉洁奉公的表率。

Leading cadres should play an exemplary role in observing discipline and the law, consciously (or readily) accept supervision and resist the corrosion of decadent ideas, setting an example of working hard and performing their official duties honestly.

领导干部要带领群众坚决同腐败现象作斗争。

Leading cadres should lead the masses in resolutely fighting corruption.

要把反腐败斗争同纯洁党的组织结合起来。

We should combine the fight against corruption with purification of Party organization.

在党内决不允许腐败分子有藏身之地

never allow corruptionists to hide themselves within the party

(六)从严治党
Be Strict with Party Members

党要管党。
(1) The Party should supervise itself.
(2) The Party should handle Party affairs.

从严治党
(1) be strict with Party members
(2) run the Party strictly
(3) tighten Party discipline

保持党的先进性和纯洁性
maintain the Party's advanced nature and purity

忘记最终实现共产主义的远大目标,不是合格的共产党员。

Those who forget our lofty goal, the ultimate realization of communism, are not qualified members of the Communist Party.

不为实现党在社会主义初级阶段的纲领努力奋斗,同样不是合格的共产党员。

Those who do not exert themselves to achieve the Party's program for the primary stage of socialism are not qualified members of the Communist Party, either.

充分发挥党员的先锋模范作用
give full play to the exemplary vanguard role of Party members

在新的历史条件下,共产党员保持先进性,要体现时代的要求。

Under the new historical conditions, to maintain their advanced nature, Party members should meet the requirements of the times.

共产党员要胸怀共产主义远大理想,带头执行党和国家现阶段的各项政策,勇于开拓,积极进取,不怕困难,不怕挫折。

Party members should have lofty communist ideals in mind, take the lead in implementing the various policies of the Party and the state for the present stage, be brave in blazing new trails, and take the initiative to make progress in defiance of difficulties and setbacks.

共产党员要诚心诚意为人民谋利益,吃苦在前,享受在后,克己奉公,多作贡献。

Party members should work for the interests of the people sincerely, be the first to endure hardships and the last to enjoy comforts, be wholeheartedly devoted to public duties and make more contributions.

共产党员要刻苦学习马克思主义理论,增强辨别是非的能力,掌握做好本职工作的知识和本领,努力创造一流的成绩。

Party members should study Marxism assiduously, enhance their ability to differentiate between right and wrong, master professional knowledge and skills necessary for their jobs and strive for outstanding achievements.

共产党员要在危急的时刻挺身而出,维护国家和人民的利益,坚决同危害人民、危害社会、危害国家的行为作斗争。

At the critical moment Party members should step forward boldly, safeguard the interests of the state and the people and resolutely combat acts harmful to the people, society and the state.

严格按党章办事,按党的制度和规定办事

act in strict accordance with the Constitution of the Party and the Party's systems and rules

对党员特别是领导干部严格要求、严格管理、严格监督

be strict with Party members, leading cadres in particular, and strictly manage and supervise them

在党内生活中讲党性,讲原则,开展积极的思想斗争,弘扬正气,反对歪风

stress Party spirit and principles, conduct active ideological struggle, encourage healthy trends and oppose unhealthy practices in inner-Party life

严格按照党章规定的标准发展党员

recruit new Party members strictly in accordance with the standards provided for by the Constitution of the Party

严肃处理不合格党员

see to it that unqualified Party members are duly dealt with

严格执行党的纪律

strictly enforce Party discipline

坚持纪律面前人人平等

ensure that all members are equal before discipline

加强党的纪律检查工作

strengthen the Party's discipline inspection work (or Party discipline inspection work)

第二部分
按汉语拼音字母顺序
排列的用语

PART TWO
Terms Arranged in the Order
of the Chinese Phonetic Alphabet

A

ài

爱国不分先后
Anyone is welcome, whether he embraces patriotism early or late.

爱国统一战线
the patriotic united front

爱国卫生运动
the patriotic health campaign

爱国一家
All patriots are of one family.

爱国者
patriot

爱国主义
patriotism

爱国主义、集体主义、社会主义教育
education in patriotism, collectivism and socialism

爱国主义教育基地
base for patriotic education

爱护儿童、教育儿童、为儿童做表率、为儿童办实事
protect and educate children, and set an example and do practical things for children

爱婴行动
baby friendly program

爱婴医院
baby friendly hospital

爱祖国、爱人民、爱劳动、爱科学、爱社会主义的公德
the civic virtues of love of the motherland, of the people, of
labor, of science and of socialism; the public morality of love
for the motherland, the people, labor, science and socialism

ān

安定团结
stability and unity

安定团结的政治局面
political stability and unity

安居工程
adequate (or comfortable) housing project(s)

安全卫生的劳动环境
safe and hygienic work environment

àn

按保护价收购农民余粮
purchase peasants' surplus grain at protective prices

按劳分配
distribution according to work

按劳分配和按生产要素分配相结合
combine remuneration according to work and remuneration according to (essential) factors of production put in

按劳分配为主体的多种分配方式
different (or diverse) modes of distribution with distribution
according to work remaining dominant

按生产要素分配

distribution according to (essential) factors of production put in

ào

奥林匹克运动会
the Olympic Games

奥运争光计划
the program of "striving for Olympic glory"

澳门回归祖国
Macao's return to the motherland

B

bǎi

百花齐放、百家争鸣的方针
the policy (or principle) of letting a hundred flowers blossom
and a hundred schools of thought contend

bàn

办学体制改革
reform of the system for running schools

办学效益
overall efficiency of schools; the efficiency in running schools

bāng

帮助经济困难的学生完成学业

help students with financial difficulties complete their study

bǎo

保持国家稳定
maintain stability of the country; maintain the country stable

保持国民经济持续、快速、健康发展
maintain sustained, rapid and sound development of the national economy

保持宏观经济稳定
maintain macro-economic stability

保持清正廉洁
remain upright, just, honest and clean

保持人民币汇率稳定
keep the exchange rates for the Renminbi (RMB) stable

保持稳定
maintain stability

保持香港长期繁荣稳定
maintain long-term prosperity and stability of Hong Kong

保持政治[社会]稳定
maintain political [social] stability

保护儿童的合法权益
protect children's lawful rights and interests

保护儿童的生存和发展
protect children's survival and development

保护妇女的权利和利益
protect the rights and interests of women

保护妇女特殊权益
protect the special rights and interests of women

保护革命文物

protect revolutionary relics

保护耕地
protect farmland (or arable land; or cultivated land)

保护公民的合法权益
protect the lawful rights and interests of citizens

保护归侨和侨眷的合法的权利和利益
protect the lawful rights and interests of returned overseas Chinese and of the family members of Chinese nationals residing abroad (or the family members of overseas Chinese)

保护海洋环境
protect the marine environment

保护合法收入
protect lawful incomes (or lawfully earned incomes)

保护华侨的正当的权利和利益
protect the legitimate rights and interests of Chinese nationals residing abroad

保护环境
protect the environment

保护婚姻、家庭
protect marriage and the family

保护科学、历史、文化的遗产
protect scientific, historical and cultural heritage

保护全球环境
protect the global environment

保护人民健康
protect the people's health

保护森林植被
protect forest vegetation

保护少数民族文化遗产
protect the cultural heritage of the ethnic minorities

保护生活环境和生态环境
protect living environment and ecological environment

保护水资源
protect water resources

保护文学和艺术[科学]作品
protect literary and artistic [scientific] works

保护在中国境内的外国人的合法权利和利益
protect the lawful rights and interests of foreigners within Chinese territory

保护珍贵的动物和植物
protect rare animals and plants

保护正常的宗教活动
protect normal religious activities

保护知识产权
protect intellectual property rights

保卫人民的和平劳动
safeguard the people's peaceful labor

保卫祖国
defend the motherland

保险(业)
insurance

保障残疾人合法权益
protect the lawful rights and interests of the disabled

保障党员的民主权利
guarantee the democratic rights of Party members (within the Party)

保障各少数民族的合法权利和利益
protect the lawful rights and interests of the ethnic minorities

保障居民基本生活需要
guarantee the basic needs of the residents

保障劳动者的安全和健康
protect workers' safety and health

保障劳动者权利
protect the rights of working people

保障老年人合法权益
protect the lawful rights and interests of the elderly

保障人民当家作主的权利
guarantee the rights of the people as the masters of the country

保障人民的人权和生命财产安全
guarantee the people's human rights and safety of lives and property

保障人民群众的民主权利
guarantee the democratic rights of the masses

保障自然资源的合理利用
ensure the rational use of natural resources

biàn

辨别是非的能力
the ability to differentiate between right and wrong

辩证唯物主义
dialectical materialism

辩证唯物主义和历史唯物主义
dialectical and historical materialism

biāo

标本兼治
seek both temporary and permanent solutions

bō

拨乱反正
set things to rights; set things right; bring order out of chaos

bó

"博爱工程"
Love of Humanity Project

博士后流动站
post-doctorate position

博士学位授予单位
unit granting doctorates

博士学位研究生
candidate for doctorate

C

cái

裁减军队员额
reduce military personnel

财政收入
fiscal revenue; revenue

财政收支结构
the revenue and expenditure structure

财政体制改革

reform of the fiscal system

财政政策和货币政策
financial and monetary policies

cài

"菜篮子"工程
"vegetable basket" project

"菜篮子"市长负责制
the system of city mayors assuming responsibility for the "vegetable basket"

cān

参政议政
participate in and deliberate state affairs; participation in and deliberation of state affairs

cán

残疾儿童的特殊教育
special education for disabled children

残疾儿童康复工作
the work for convalescence of disabled children; rehabilitation work for disabled children

残疾人教育
disabled persons' education; education for the disabled

残疾人事业
the cause for disabled persons (or the disabled)

残疾预防和康复
disability prevention and rehabilitation

cǎo

草地建设
grassland construction

草地资源的保护和管理
protection and management of grassland resources

草原管理
grassland administration

chá

查处大案要案
investigate and deal with major cases

chǎn

产品结构
the mix of products; product mix

产品质量
the quality of products

产权
property right; ownership

产权清晰
clearly established ownership

产学研结合
combining production, teaching and research; the combination of production, teaching and research

产学研联合
production units-educational institutions-research institutes association

产业结构
the structure of production; industrial structure

产业升级
upgrading industries; industrial upgrading

cháng

长江三角洲和整个长江流域
the Yangtze River Delta and the whole Yangtze River basin

长江三峡水利枢纽工程
the key Yangtze Three Gorges water conservancy project

"长期共存、互相监督、肝胆相照、荣辱与共"的方针
the principle of "long-term coexistence, mutual supervision, treating each other with all sincerity and sharing weal or woe"

chǎng

厂长[经理]负责制
the system under which the factory director [the manager] assumes full responsibility

chéng

成人高等学校
adult higher learning institutes; institutions of higher learning for adults

成人教育
adult education

成人中等学校
adult secondary school

承包经营
contract operation

城市改革
urban reform

城市功能布局
layout of urban functions

城市化
urbanization

城市环境综合整治
comprehensive improvement of urban environment

城市教育费附加
(government-controlled) added city education fund

城市居民委员会
urban neighborhood committee; urban residents' committee

城市绿化
urban afforestation

城乡居民储蓄存款
savings deposits of urban and rural residents

城乡居民的营养状况
the diet (or nutritional status) of urban and rural residents

城乡居民实际收入
the real income of the residents (or the people) in both urban and rural areas

城镇居民人均生活费收入
the (average annual) per-capita income for living expenses of urban dwellers

城镇居民人均消费支出
the per-capita consumption expenses of urban dwellers

城镇居民自治制度
the system of self-government of urban residents

程控自动电话交换机
program-controlled telephone switchboard

chī

吃苦在前,享受在后
be the first to endure (or bear) hardships and the last to enjoy comforts

chū

出口退税制度
the system of export tax refunds

chuāng

"窗口行业"
"window trades"

chuàng

创新
innovation; creation; creation and innovation; creating and innovating; creativity

创造性
creativity; creativeness

chún

纯洁党的组织
purify Party organization

cóng

从计划经济体制向社会主义市场经济体制的转变
the shift from a planned economy to a socialist market economy

从严治党
be strict with Party members; run the Party strictly; tighten
Party discipline

从严治军
be strict with the army

cù

促进发展
promote development

促进人类进步事业
promote the cause of human progress

促进人类的和平和发展
promote peace and development for all mankind

cūn

村民委员会
villagers' committee; village committee

村民自治制度
the system of self-government of villagers (or of village people)

村务公开
publicize village affairs; make public village affairs (to the villagers)

村镇文化

village and township culture

D

dǎ

打击犯罪活动
crack down on crime

打击经济犯罪
crack down on economic crime

打击生产销售盗版制品活动
deal a heavy blow to the production and selling of pirated products

打击刑事犯罪活动
crack down on criminal offences

打击走私
crack down on smuggling

dà

大公无私
be selfless and completely devoted to the public interest; selfless

大局
overall (or general) situation; overall interests

大气污染防治
prevention and control of air pollution

大专院校

universities and colleges; institutions of higher learning

dài

贷学金
loan for students; student loans

带薪年休假制度
a paid annual vacation system

dàn

淡水资源
freshwater resources

dǎng

党代表大会制度
the system of Party congresses

党的工人阶级先锋队性质
the nature of the Party as the vanguard of the working class;
the Party's nature of being the vanguard of the working class

党的基本方针
the Party's basic principle

党(在社会主义初级阶段)的基本纲领
the Party's basic program (for the primary stage of socialism)

党的基本理论
the Party's basic theory

党(在社会主义初级阶段)的基本路线
the Party's basic line (for the primary stage of socialism)

党的基层组织
grassroots (or primary) Party organizations

党的纪律
Party discipline

党的纪律检查工作
the Party's discipline inspection work; Party discipline inspection work

党的建设
Party building

党的领导
the leadership of (or by) the Party; Party leadership

党的路线方针政策
the Party's line, principles and policies

党的民族政策
the Party's policies toward ethnic minorities; the Party's policy toward nationalities

党的凝聚力和战斗力
the Party's cohesiveness and fighting capacity

党的农村基本政策
the Party's basic rural policies

党的侨务政策
the Party's policy concerning overseas Chinese affairs

党的全心全意为人民服务的宗旨
the Party's aim (or purpose) of serving the people wholeheartedly

党的三大作风
the Party's three important (or major) styles of work; the three major features of the Party's style of work (i.e. integrating theory with practice, forging close links with the masses and practicing self-criticism)

党的团结和统一
the Party's unity and unification

党的先进性和纯洁性

the Party's advanced nature and purity; the Party's advanced and pure nature

党的优良传统
the Party's fine traditions

党的政策
the Party's policies

党的知识分子政策
the Party's policy toward intellectuals

党的指导思想
the Party's guiding ideology

党的宗教政策
the Party's policy concerning religion

党的组织原则
the Party's organizational principle

党的最终目标——实现共产主义的社会制度
the Party's ultimate goal—the creation of a communist social system

党风
the Party's style of work; the Party's work style; Party conduct

党风建设
improving the Party's style of work; the building of a fine Party style of work; the improvement of the Party's work style

党和国家领导制度的改革
reform of the system of Party and state leadership

党际关系四项原则(独立自主,完全平等,互相尊重,互不干涉内部事务)
the four principles for inter-party relations (i. e. independence, complete equality, mutual respect and non-interference in each other's internal affairs)

党内监督
supervision within the Party; supervision by Party (organiza-

tions and) members; inner-Party supervision

党内民主
inner-Party democracy

党内生活
inner-Party activities

党委集体领导制度
the system of collective leadership by Party committee(s)

党委集体领导和个人分工负责相结合的制度
the system of combining collective leadership by Party committees and division of labor with individual responsibility; the system whereby the collective leadership by Party committees at all levels is combined with division of work and individual responsibility

党性
Party spirit

党性党风教育
education in Party spirit and conduct

"党要管党"的原则
the principle that the Party should supervise itself; the principle that the Party should handle Party affairs

党员的先锋模范作用
the exemplary vanguard role of Party members; the vanguard and exemplary role of Party members

党政机关
Party and government organs

党政领导机关
leading organs of the Party and government

党支部的战斗堡垒作用
the role of the Party branch as a powerful force (or a fighting bastion)

dé

德才兼备的原则
the principle of having both ability and political integrity (or both political integrity and professional competence)

德育
moral education; moral culture

德智体(等)全面发展
develop morally, intellectually and physically in an all-round way; an all-round development in moral, intellectual, physical and other aspects

dèng

邓小平理论
Deng Xiaoping Theory

邓小平理论的科学体系和精神实质
the scientific system and the essence of Deng Xiaoping Theory

邓小平理论的历史地位和指导意义
historical status and guiding significance of Deng Xiaoping Theory

dǐ

抵抗侵略
resist aggression

抵御敌对势力对我"西化"、"分化"的图谋
resist the conspiracy by hostile forces to westernize and split our country

抵御封建主义、资本主义腐朽思想的侵蚀
resist the corrosion of decadent feudal (or feudalistic) and cap-

italist ideas

dì

地区发展差距
regional development disparities; regional disparities (or gaps) in development; the gap(s) in development between different regions

地区经济合理布局和协调发展
rational distribution and coordinated development of regional economies

地质勘探
geological prospecting; geological exploration

第二步战略目标
strategic objective of the second step

第二产业
secondary industry

第三步战略目标
strategic objective of the third step

第三产业
tertiary industry

第三代[第二代]领导集体
the third [the second] generation of collective leadership

第三世界
the Third World

第三世界国家
the Third World countries

第一产业
primary industry

第一生产力
primary productive force

diàn

电力工业
(electric) power industry

电气化铁路
electric railway

电信
telecommunications

电子工业
electronics industry

电子计算机
electronic computer

电子商务
electronic business; electronic commerce

电子信息技术
electron-information technology; electronic information technology

电子元器件及其生产检测设备
electronic components and related manufacturing and testing equipment

diào

调动广大农民的积极性
arouse (or mobilize, or stimulate) the enthusiasm of the broad masses of the peasants

调动人民群众的积极性
arouse (or mobilize, or stimulate) the enthusiasm of the masses (or of the people)

调动一切积极因素

bring every positive factor into play

dōng

东部地区
eastern part of the country; eastern regions

东部沿海地区
the coastal region in east China; eastern coastal areas

dú

独立自主的和平外交政策
independent foreign policy of peace

duì

对党员[领导干部]严格要求、严格管理、严格监督
be strict with Party members [leading cadres] and strictly manage and supervise them

对外经济、技术合作与交流
economic and technological cooperation and exchanges with foreign (or other) countries

对外经济贸易体制改革
reform of the system of trade and economic relations with foreign countries

对外开放
opening to the outside world; opening-up; opening up

对外贸易
foreign trade; external trade

对外商投资企业实行国民待遇
grant foreign-funded enterprises the same treatment as their Chinese counterparts

对外投资
investment abroad; invest abroad

对外文化交流
cultural exchange with foreign countries

对外政策
foreign policy

对行政工作人员的监察
supervision over administrative personnel

对罪犯的劳动改造
reform of criminals through labor

对罪犯的刑罚执行
carrying out the punishment of criminals

对罪犯的依法文明管理
humane handling of prisoners in accordance with the law

对罪犯的法制、道德、文化和技术教育
legal, moral, cultural and technical education of criminals

对罪犯的感化
changing criminals through methods of persuasion

duō

多边外交活动
multilateral diplomatic activities

多党合作
multi-party cooperation

多极化趋势
the trend (or tendency) toward multi-polarity; trend of multi-polarization; multi-polar trend

多渠道筹措教育经费
raise educational funds through various channels

多渠道转移农业富余劳动力
transfer surplus rural labor force through diversified channels

多元化投资主体
a diversity of (major) investors

多种经济成分
diversified economic sectors; diverse sectors of the economy

多种经营
diversified economy

多种所有制经济
different types (or diverse forms) of ownership; economic sectors under diversified ownership

E

è

遏制国际游资的过度投机
contain over-speculation of international hot money

ēn

"恩格尔系数"
the Engel's coefficient

ér

儿童的健康与保健
children's health and care

儿童的生存、保护和发展
children's survival, protection and development; the survival, protection and development of children

儿童的医疗保健
medical care for children

儿童发展规划
development plan for children

儿童发展目标
goals for children's development

儿童福利院
welfare home for children

儿童计划免疫工作
work on (or of) planned immunity for children

儿童教育事业
children's education; education for children

儿童科学膳食制度
a scientific diet for children

《儿童权利公约》
Convention on the Rights of Children

《儿童生存、保护和发展世界宣言》
World Declaration on the Survival, Protection and Development of Children

儿童生长发育图
a chart to monitor children's natural growth

儿童预防接种率
the rate of inoculated children

èr

200 海里专属经济区和大陆架的主权权利和管辖权
sovereignty and jurisdiction over the EEZs (i.e. exclusive eco-

nomic zones) and continental shelves up to 200 nautical miles
off the coasts

F

fā

发达国家
developed country

发电装机容量
(installed) power-generating capacity

发明创造
inventions and other creations; innovations and inventions

发展教育科学文化
develop education, science and culture; develop education,
science and cultural undertakings

发展经济
develop (or expand) the economy

发展科学技术
develop science and technology; promote the development of
science and technology

发展社会主义民主
develop socialist democracy

发展生产力
develop the productive forces

发展体育事业
develop physical culture; promote sports

发展体育运动

develop physical culture and sports

发展中国家
developing country

fǎ

法律监督
supervision by the law

法律面前人人平等
All are equal before the law.

法律体系
a legal system; a statutory framework

法律援助(基金)
legal assistance(fund)

法人实体
corporate entity

法治原则
principle of the rule of law

法制观念
awareness of the importance of the legal system

法制建设
improvement(or development)of the legal system; strengthening(or improving)the legal system

fán

繁荣昌盛
thriving and prosperous

繁荣社会主义文化
promote a flourishing socialist culture

繁荣文学艺术
boost literature and art; promote a flourishing literature and art; enable literature and art to flourish

繁荣学术
boost academic activities

fǎn

反对霸权主义、强权政治
oppose (or combat) hegemonism and power politics

反对拜金主义、享乐主义、个人主义
oppose (or combat) money worship, hedonism (or pleasure seeking) and individualism

反对崇洋媚外
oppose worshipping foreign things and toadying to foreign powers

反对动辄进行制裁或以制裁相威胁
be opposed to imposing or threatening to impose sanctions without good reason

反对分裂，反对"台独"，反对制造"两个中国"、"一中一台"
oppose splitting, the "independence of Taiwan", the attempt to create "two Chinas" or "one China and one Taiwan"

反对封建迷信活动
oppose feudal superstitious activities; combat feudal and superstitious activities

反对官僚主义
combat bureaucracy (or bureaucratism)

反对核讹诈和核威慑政策
oppose nuclear blackmail and the nuclear deterrent policy

反对假冒伪劣、欺诈行为
fight against counterfeit goods and frauds and cheating; fight

against fake or poor goods（or fake or shoddy goods）and cheating actions

反对军备竞赛
oppose the arms race

反对浪费
combat waste

反对利用人权等问题干涉别国内政
oppose the use of human rights and other issues to interfere in the internal affairs of other countries

反对利用宗教干涉别国内政
oppose interfering in the internal affairs of other countries under the pretext of religion

反对利用宗教进行非法活动和恐怖主义活动
oppose attempts to engage in illegal activities and terrorist actions under the signboard of religion

反对民族分裂
oppose national separation

反对民族分裂主义
oppose national splittism

反对任人唯亲
oppose appointing people by favoritism

反对外国势力干涉中国统一
oppose any interference in China's reunification by foreign forces

反对外空军备竞赛
oppose the arms race in outer space

反对小团体主义、本位主义
oppose（or combat）petty cliquism（or small group mentality）and departmental selfishness

反对在国家关系中诉诸武力或以武力相威胁
oppose the use of force or the threat of force in international re-

lations; oppose resorting to force or the threat of force in international relations

反对资产阶级自由化

combat (or oppose, or struggle against) bourgeois liberalization

反腐败斗争

the fight against corruption; anti-corruption struggle; combating corruption

反腐倡廉

combat corruption and advocate a clean (or an honest and clean) government

反映社会化生产规律的经营方式和组织形式

management methods and organizational forms that mirror the laws governing socialized production

fáng

防范和化解金融风险

guard against and eliminate financial risks

防洪

prevent (or control) floods; flood prevention (or control)

防洪治涝

flood prevention and water-logging control

防护林体系工程

shelterbelts project(s)

防卫作战能力

defense capabilities; defense capabilities and combat effectiveness

防汛抗旱

flood control and drought relief

防止大规模杀伤性武器的扩散

prevent the proliferation (or spread) of weapons of mass destruction

防止核武器扩散
prevent the proliferation (or spread) of nuclear weapons

防止和平演变
prevent peaceful evolution toward capitalism

防治草场退化
prevent and control grassland deterioration

防治工业污染
prevent and control industrial pollution

防治荒漠化
prevent and control (or battle) desertification

防治噪声污染
prevent and control noise pollution

房地产市场
real estate market

fàng

放活国有小型企业
adopt a flexible policy toward small state-owned enterprises

放射性同位素与射线装置发射防护
prevention of and protection against radiation from radioisotopes and radioactive device

fēi

非党干部
non-Party cadres

非公有制经济
non-public sector of the economy

fēi

废除干部领导职务终身制
abolish cadres' life-long tenure system; abolish the system of cadres' life-long tenure in leading posts

fēn

分配结构和分配方式
the structure and mode of distribution

分配制度改革
reform of the distribution system（or the system for distribution）

分三步走基本实现现代化的发展战略
the development strategy for the basic realization of modernization in three steps（or in three stages）

分税制
revenue-sharing system; a system of tax distribution

分析问题和解决问题的能力
the ability to analyze and solve problems

fú

扶贫
assist poverty-stricken people（or indigent people）; assist poverty-stricken areas（or poor areas）; help the poor; aid-the-poor

扶贫攻坚
fighting poverty

扶贫开发
anti-poverty development

服从和服务于国家经济建设大局
be subordinated to and serve the overall (or general) interest(s)
of national economic development

服务领域的对外开放
opening to the outside world in service sectors

服务贸易
service trade

服务行业承诺制
system of offering guarantees to consumers in service industry
(or service trades)

服务性消费
service consumption

服务业
service industry; service trades; services

fù

妇女的生育自主权
women's right to decide whether or not to bear children

妇女儿童的医疗卫生保健工作
the medical and health care of women and children

妇女解放
female emancipation; emancipation of women

妇女解放运动
women's liberation movement

妇幼保健事业
health care for women and children; maternal and child health
care

妇幼保健院
maternity and children's health care center

妇幼卫生服务体系

a maternity and child hygiene service system

妇女联合会
the women's federation

妇女干部
women cadres

富强民主文明的社会主义国家
a prosperous, strong, democratic and culturally advanced socialist country; a socialist country which is prosperous, strong, democratic and civilized

富裕民主文明的社会主义新农村
a new socialist countryside which is wealthy, democratic and civilized

G

gǎi

改革开放
reform and opening up; reform and opening-up; reform and opening to the outside world

改善劳动条件
improve work conditions

改造和提高传统产业
transform and upgrade traditional industries

改造客观世界
transform the objective world

改造中低产田
transform (or upgrade) medium- and low-yield fields

改造主观世界
transform the subjective world

改造罪犯的工作
criminal reform; reform of criminals

gàn

干部队伍"革命化、年轻化、知识化、专业化"的方针
the principle of making the contingent (or ranks) of cadres
more revolutionary, younger, better educated and more competent professionally

干部交流
exchange(s) of cadres; transferring cadres from one job to another as appropriate

干部教育培训
the education and training of the cadres

干部考核
assessment of cadres

干部人事制度改革
reform of the personnel system relating to cadres

干部(离)退休制度
cadre retirement system

干部要能上能下
see that our cadres are ready to go up and equally ready to
come down; see that our cadres are ready to take a lower as
well as a higher post

干部制度改革
reform of the cadre(s) system

gāng

钢铁工业
iron and steel industry

港澳同胞
compatriots in Hong Kong and Macao

"港人治港"
"Hong Kong people administering Hong Kong"

gāo

高产优质高效农业
an agriculture featuring high yields, fine quality and high efficiency

高等教育
higher education

高等教育管理体制改革
reform of the management system of higher education

高等教育自学考试
higher education examinations for self-study students

高等学校
institutions of higher learning; universities and colleges

高等学校财政拨款机制改革
reform of the financial allocation mechanism for institutions of higher learning

高等学校招生制度改革
reform of the enrollment system of institutions of higher learning

高等学校毕业生就业制度改革
reform of the employment system for graduates from universi-

ties and colleges

高度自治
a high degree of autonomy

高附加值产品
product of high added-value

高技术（高科技）
high technology; high-tech

高技术产业
high-tech industries

高举邓小平理论伟大旗帜
hold high the great banner of Deng Xiaoping Theory

高能物理
high-energy physics

高素质的干部队伍
a contingent of highly qualified cadres; a high-quality contingent of cadres

高素质的劳动者
qualified laborers

高速公路
expressway; freeway

高新技术
high and new technology (or technologies)

高增长、低通胀的良好发展势头
good momentum of development featuring high economic growth and low inflation

gé

革命传统
revolutionary traditions

革命化
revolutionize; be more revolutionary

革命化、现代化、正规化的人民军队
a revolutionary, modernized and standardized (or regularized)
people's army

gè

个体经济
individual economy

各级政府[党委,领导干部]
governments [Party committees, leading cadres] at all levels

各民族的平等、团结、互助关系
relationship of equality, unity and mutual assistance among all
(of China's) nationalities

gēng

耕地总量的动态平衡
the dynamic equilibrium of the total cultivated land

gōng

工会
trade union

工农联盟
alliance of workers and peasants; worker-peasant alliance

工人阶级领导
the leadership of the working class

工伤保险
industrial injury insurance; insurance against injury at work

工商行政管理部门
the administrative department for industry and commerce

工商业联合会
association (or federation) of industry and commerce

工业布局
industrial distribution

工业产权
industrial property (rights)

工业化
industrialization

工业化国家
industrial country; industrialized country

工业"三废"的处理和综合利用
treatment and comprehensive utilization of the industrial "three wastes" (i.e. waste gas, waste water and waste industrial residue)

工业现代化
modernization of industry

工业增加值
the added value of industry

工业总产值
the total output value of industry

工资制度改革
reform of the salary (or wage) system

公安部门
public security department

公共积累
public accumulation

公共设施
public facilities

公共文化[福利]设施
public cultural [welfare] facilities

公开办事制度
an open administrative system

公路干线
trunk highway

公民的基本权利和义务
the fundamental rights and duties of citizens

公民的劳动的权利和义务
citizens' right and duty to work

公民的劳动权和劳动者权益的保障
the protection of the right of citizens to work and the rights and interests of workers

公民的民主权利
citizens' democratic rights

公民的受教育的权利和义务
citizens' right and duty to receive education

公民的选举权和被选举权
citizens' right to vote and stand for election

《公民权利和政治权利国际公约》
International Covenant on Civil and Political Rights

公平竞争
fair competition

公司制
corporate system

公务员制度
system of public servants (or civil servants); system of public service (or civil service); public service (or civil service) system

公有制

public ownership

公有制的主体地位
the dominant position of public ownership

公有制经济的主体作用
the dominant role of the public sector of the economy

公有制的多种实现形式
various forms for materializing (or realizing) public ownership

公有资本的支配范围
the area of control by public capital

公有资产
public assets

供求关系
relation(s) between supply and demand

供求平衡
a balance between supply and demand

供销合作社
supply and marketing cooperative

gòng

共产党的领导
the leadership of (or by) the Communist Party

共产党领导的多党合作和政治协商制度
the system of multi-party cooperation and political consultation
under the leadership of the Communist Party

共产党同党外人士的联盟
the alliance of the Communist Party with non-Party people

共产党同民主党派合作共事
the cooperation of the Communist Party with the democratic
parties

《共产党宣言》
Manifesto of the Communist Party

共产主义理想
communist ideals

共产主义思想和共产主义道德
communist ideology and ethics

共产主义信念
communist conviction; faith (or belief) in communism

共同富裕
common prosperity

共同理想
common ideals

gū

孤儿福利基金
welfare funds for orphans

孤儿监护养育
rearing under guardianship offered to orphans

gǔ

股份制
joint stock system; joint share system; shareholding system

股份合作制
joint stock cooperative system; joint stock partnership

鼓励创造发明
encourage people to be creative and inventive

鼓励(企业)兼并
encourage merger (of enterprises)

gù

固定资产投资
investment in fixed assets

固体废物污染环境防治
prevention and control of environmental pollution by solid wastes

guān

关税总水平
the general level of tariffs; overall tariff rate

关心下岗职工的生活
be concerned with the well-being of the laid-off workers

关心下一代工作委员会
Working Committee for the Care of the Next Generation

guǎn

管理国家事务
administer state affairs

管理经济文化事业
manage economic and cultural undertakings

管理经验
management expertise; managerial expertise

"管理培训工程"
"management training project"

管理社会事务
manage social affairs

guāng

光纤通信线路
optical fiber telecommunications line

guǎng

广播电视网
a broadcasting and television network

广播影视
radio, film and television

guī

规范和维护金融秩序
standardize and safeguard the financial order

规范破产
standardize bankruptcy procedures

规范市场行为
standardize market activities

规模经济
economy of scale

guó

国防动员体制
mobilization system for national defense

国防费
defense expenditure; expenditure on national defense

国防工业

defense industry

国防后备力量
the reserves for national defense; the reserve force for defense

国防建设
national defense construction; the work in defense

国防教育
education about national defense; defense education

国防科技工业
defense technology industry

国防科技研究
research in defense-related science and technology; scientific and technological research for national defense; defense research

国防现代化
modernization of national defense

国际安全合作
international security cooperation

国际法基本准则
the basic norms of international law; the basic international legal norms

国际关系准则
norms of international relations; international relationship norms; standards for international relations

国际惯例
international practice; usual international practice

国际海底资源的和平利用
the peaceful utilization of international seabed resources

国际货币基金组织
International Monetary Fund（IMF）

国际教育［科学，文化］合作与交流

international educational〔scientific, cultural〕cooperation and exchange

国际经济合作
international economic cooperation

国际经济技术合作与交流
international economic and technological cooperation and exchanges

国际经济竞争
international economic competition

国际经济通行规则
generally accepted international practices in the economic field

国际竞争力
international competitiveness

国际社会
international community

国际市场
international market(s)

国际形势
international situation

国际政治经济新秩序
new international political and economic order

国际主义
internationalism

国家安全
state (or national) security

国家安全部门
state security department

国家财政
state finance

国家产业政策

state（or national）industrial policy（or policies）

国家长治久安
long-term（peace and）stability of the country; lasting political stability of the country; long-term security and order of the state

国家创新能力
national innovating capacity

国家创新体系
national innovation system

国家对农业的支持和保护体系
a system of the state for supporting and protecting agriculture; a system of state support and protection for agriculture

国家高新技术产业开发区
national high and new technology industrial development zone

国家计划
state plan

国家计划的宏观性、战略性和政策性
the macro-economic, strategic and policy-related characteristics of the state plan

国家技术发明奖
national technical invention award

国家金融安全
the financial security of the country

国家经济安全
the economic security of the country

国家经济建设大局
the overall interests of national economic development

国家科技进步奖
national scientific and technological progress award; national award for progress in science and technology

国家权力机关
the organs of state power

国家税收
state tax receipts; state tax revenue

国家统一
unification of the country; national unification

国家外汇储备
state (or national) foreign exchange reserves

国家行政[审判,检察]机关
administrative [judicial, procuratorial] organs of the state

国家知识创新体系
national knowledge-innovation system

国家重点建设项目
state (or national) key construction project

国家自然科学奖
national natural science award

国民经济
national economy

国民经济命脉
the life-blood of the national economy

国民经济市场化进程
the process of building a complete market system in the national economy; the market-oriented process of the national economy

国民经济信息化
extension of the use of information technology in national economy development; informationizing the national economy

国民经济整体素质和效益
the quality and performance of the national economy as a whole; the overall quality and performance of the national economy

国民生产总值
gross national product (GNP)

国内国外两个市场、两种资源
both Chinese (or domestic) and foreign markets and resources

国内生产总值
gross domestic product (GDP)

国内市场
domestic market(s)

国内需求
domestic demand

国情
national conditions

国情教育
education about national conditions

国土整治
territorial control

国土资源
land and resources

国土资源开发和整治
the development and improvement of our land and resources

国务院总理
Premier of the State Council

国有大型[中型,小型]企业
large [medium-sized, small] state-owned enterprise

国有大型企业集团
large state-owned enterprise group

国有经济
state-owned sector of the economy; state-owned economy

国有经济布局
the pattern (or distribution) of the state-owned sector of the

economy

国有经济的控制力
the control power of the state-owned sector of the economy

国有经济的主导作用
the leading role of the state-owned sector of the economy

国有控股企业
state-holding enterprise

国有企业
state-owned enterprise

国有企业党组织的政治核心作用
the role of Party organizations as the political nuclei in state-owned enterprises

国有企业的改革和发展
the reform and development of state-owned enterprises

国有企业的(技术)改造
(technical) upgrading (or transformation) of state-owned enterprises

国有企业的(战略性)改组
(strategic) reorganization of state-owned enterprises

国有资产
state-owned assets; state assets

国有资产保值增值
preservation and increment of the value of state assets; preserving and increasing the value of state assets

国有资产管理、监督和营运机制
a mechanism for the management, supervision and operation of state assets

国有资产管理体制改革
reform of the management system for state assets

H

hǎi

海岸带的综合开发和管理
comprehensive development and administration of the coastal
zones

海上安全
maritime safety

海水淡化
seawater desalination

海水直接利用
direct seawater utilization

海水综合利用
comprehensive utilization of seawater

海外侨胞、华人
overseas Chinese and people of Chinese descent

海峡两岸
the two sides of the (Taiwan) Straits

海峡两岸关系
relations between the two sides of the Taiwan Straits; relations
across Taiwan Straits; inter-Straits relations

海峡两岸关系协会
Association for Relations Across the Taiwan Straits

海洋产业
marine industries

海洋的开发和保护
marine development and protection; exploitation and protection

of the ocean

海洋的开发和整治
marine development and control

海洋调查和科学考察
oceanographic survey and research

海洋防灾减灾
marine disaster prevention and reduction

海洋高技术研究
marine high-tech research

海洋管辖权
marine jurisdiction

海洋环境的保护和保全
the protection and preservation of the marine environment

海洋环境监测、监视和执法管理
the monitoring, surveillance, law enforcement and management of the marine environment

海洋监测技术
marine monitoring technologies

海洋交通运输
maritime transportation

海洋经济
marine economy

海洋科技产业化
the application of oceanographic technologies to marine industries

海洋科学技术和教育
oceanographic science, technology and education

海洋可持续发展战略
sustainable marine development strategy

海洋可再生能源

regenerable marine energy

海洋旅游业
marine tourism

海洋能发电
power generation with marine energy

海洋能利用
exploitation of marine energy

海洋倾废管理
the control of marine wastes dumping

海洋生态环境
the marine eco-environment

海洋生物资源深加工技术
technology of fine processing of marine biological resources

海洋石油勘探开发
offshore oil exploration and exploitation

海洋石油天然气产业
offshore oil and natural gas industry

海洋石油资源
offshore petroleum resources

海洋事务的国际合作
international cooperation in maritime affairs

海洋污染防治
prevention and control of marine pollution

海洋医药业
marine pharmaceutical industry

海洋渔业
ocean fishing industry

海洋资源保护
the protection of marine resources

海洋资源的开发利用
the development and utilization of marine resources

海洋资源的可持续利用
the sustainable utilization of marine resources

海洋自然保护区
marine nature reserve

海洋综合管理
comprehensive marine management

háng

航空工程
aeronautical engineering

航空工业
aviation industry

航空学
aeronautics

航天工业
aerospace industry

航天技术
space technology

航天学
astronautics

航运
shipping

hé

核裁军
nuclear disarmament

核电站
nuclear power plant

核电行业
nuclear power industry

核能和平利用
peaceful use (or utilization) of nuclear energy

核能技术
nuclear energy technology

合法权益
lawful rights and interests

合伙企业
enterprise in partnership; partnership enterprise

合理配置教育资源
judiciously allocate resources for education

合资企业
joint venture

合作经济组织
cooperative economic organization (or entity)

合作经营
joint operation; cooperative operation

合作企业
cooperative venture; cooperative enterprise

和平共处
peaceful coexistence

和平共处五项原则
the Five Principles of Peaceful Coexistence (i. e. mutual respect for sovereignty and territorial integrity, mutual non-aggression, non-interference in each other's internal affairs, equality and mutual benefit, and peaceful coexistence)

和平国际环境

peaceful international environment

和平和发展的崇高事业
the lofty cause of peace and development

和平和发展的时代潮流
the trend of the times to seek peace and development

"和平统一、一国两制"的方针
the principle of "peaceful reunification and one country, two systems"

和为贵
Peace is the best option.

hàn

捍卫国家领土、领空、领海主权和海洋权益
defend the nation's sovereignty over its territorial land, air and seas as well as its marine rights and interests

旱作农业
dry-land farming

hóng

宏观经济管理
management of the overall economy; macroeconomic management

宏观调控
macroeconomic control; macro-control

弘扬万众一心、众志成城,不怕困难、顽强拼搏,坚韧不拔、敢于胜利的精神
carry forward the spirit of unity and solidarity, working with one mind and one will, of tenacious and hard struggle, fearing no difficulties, and of firmness and fortitude, daring to win victory

弘扬正气,反对歪风
encourage healthy trends and oppose unhealthy practices

弘扬主旋律,提倡多样化
give full scope to the theme of our times while advocating diversity

huán

环渤海地区
the rim of Bohai Bay; areas around the perimeter of Bohai Bay

环境保护
environmental protection

环境保护产业
environmental protection industries

环境标志
environmental label

环境标志认证
environmental label certification

环境标准
environmental standards

环境法律体系
environmental statutory framework

环境管理
environmental administration; environmental management

环境基础标准
basic environmental criteria

环境监督管理
environmental supervision and administration

环境建设
environmental improvement; environmental construction

环境科技
environmental science and technology

环境立法[执法]
environmental legislation [law enforcement]

环境污染的治理
the control of environmental pollution

环境效益
environmental benefits

环境宣传教育
environmental publicity and education

环境意识
awareness of the importance of the environment

环境影响评价制度
environmental impact assessment system

环境整治
environmental control

环境质量
the quality of environment; environmental quality

环境质量标准
environmental quality standards

huī

恢复对香港[澳门]行使主权
resume the exercise of sovereignty over Hong Kong [Macao]

hùn

混合所有制经济
the economic sector of mixed ownership

混合所有制经济中的国有成分和集体成分
the state-owned and collectively-owned elements in the economic sector of mixed ownership

J

jī

机构改革
reform of the organizational structure; institutional restructuring

机械工业
machine-building industry

积极的思想斗争
active ideological struggle

积极防御的军事战略方针
military strategy of active defense

积极探索
try to explore new ways; enthusiastic exploration

基本国策
basic state policy

基本建设
capital construction

基本经济制度
basic economic system

基本农田保护制度
the basic farmland protection system

基本养老金正常调整机制
a mechanism for regular adjustment of basic pensions

基本知识、基本理论和基本技能的培养和训练
the training (of students) in elementary knowledge, basic theories and basic skills

基层民主
democracy at the grassroots level

基层群众性自治组织
grassroots self-governing mass organizations; grassroots mass self-government organizations; mass organizations of self-management at the grassroots level

基层政权机关
the grassroots organs of state (or political) power

基层政权建设
strengthening political power at the grassroots level

基础工业
basic industries

基础教育
basic education

基础设施建设
infrastructure construction

基础性研究
basic research

激励［制约］机制
incentive [control] mechanism

jí

集成电路技术与设备
technology and equipment for integrated circuits

集体经济（集体所有制经济 ）
collective economy; collectively-owned sector of the economy

集体经济实力
the strength of the collective economy; the strength of economic collectives

集体经济组织
economic collective

集体所有制
collective ownership

集体主义
collectivism

jì

计划生育
family planning

计划生育服务网络
family planning service network

计算机软件
computer software

计算机应用
computer utility; computer application

纪律和法制教育
education in discipline and legality

纪律检查
discipline inspection

纪律检查委员会
commission for discipline inspection

纪律面前人人平等
All members are equal before discipline.

技工学校
skilled worker school

技能开发
skills development

技术创新
technology innovation

技术发明
technological (or technical) invention

技术服务
technical service

技术改造
technical (or technological) transformation (or upgrading)

技术合同
technology contract

技术进步
technological progress

技术开发
technological development

技术贸易
technology trade

技术密集型产业
technology-intensive industries

技术市场
technology market

技术转让
technology transfer

继承革命传统
carry on (or carry forward) revolutionary traditions

继承历史文化优秀传统
carry on the fine cultural traditions handed down from history;
carry on the fine historical and cultural traditions

继承和发扬中国共产党［中华民族］的优良传统

carry forward and develop the fine traditions of the Chinese Communist Party [the Chinese nation]

jiā

加工工业
processing industry

加工贸易
processing trade

加强党的建设
strengthen Party building

加强党的思想建设
strengthen Party building ideologically

加强党的组织建设
strengthen Party building organizationally

加强党的作风建设
improve the Party's style of work

加强党风廉政建设
improve the Party' style of work and strengthen the building of a clean government; redouble our efforts to improve the Party's work style and build an honest and clean government

加强和改善党的领导
strengthen and improve the leadership of the Party

加强基层民主建设
improve democracy at the grassroots level

加强军队质量建设
improve the quality of the army

加强民主法制建设
strengthen democracy and the legal system

加强民族团结
strengthen the unity of the nationalities

加强农业基础地位
strengthen agriculture as the foundation of the economy

加强勤政廉政建设
make greater efforts to keep government functionaries honest
and industrious; make greater efforts to build an honest, clean
and industrious government; step up the building of an honest
(or a clean) and industrious government

加强社会主义精神文明建设
promote socialist cultural and ideological progress

加强思想政治工作
strengthen ideological and political work

加强执法检查监督工作
tighten inspection of and supervision over law enforcement

家庭承包经营
household contract operation

家庭联产承包责任制
household responsibility contract system (or household contract
responsibility system) with remuneration linked to output

家庭美德
family virtues; family ethics

家务劳动社会化
the socialization of housework

家用电器
electrical household appliances

jià

价格改革
reform of the pricing system; price reform

价格形成机制

the mechanism for pricing

价值观
values

价值规律
the law of value

jiān

尖端科学技术领域
frontiers of science and technology

坚持党的基本路线
adhere to the Party's basic line

坚持改革开放
persevere in reform and opening up (or opening to the outside world)

坚持四项基本原则
uphold (or adhere to) the Four Cardinal Principles

坚持真理,修正错误
uphold truth, correct errors

坚定社会主义、共产主义信念
acquire (or have) a firm faith in socialism and communism

坚定正确的政治方向
firm and correct political orientation

艰苦创业
work hard with a pioneering spirit; work hard and with a pioneering spirit; start undertakings with painstaking efforts

艰苦创业精神
hardworking and enterprising spirit; hardworking and pioneering spirit

艰苦奋斗
hard struggle; hard work; work hard

艰苦奋斗的创业精神
pioneering spirit of hard struggle

艰苦奋斗的作风[传统]
the style [tradition] of hard struggle

艰苦朴素的工作作风
the style of hard work and plain living

监督
supervision

jiǎn

检察工作
procuratorial work

检察机关
procuratorial organ

减轻农民负担
lighten the burden on peasants; lighten the peasants' burdens

减轻企业负担
lighten the burden on enterprises

减少温室气体的排放
reduce the green-house gas emission

减员增效
increase efficiency by downsizing staff

减灾
disaster reduction; disaster alleviation

jiàn

建设有中国特色的社会主义
build socialism with Chinese characteristics

建设有中国特色社会主义的道路[理论,事业]
the road [theory, cause] of building socialism with Chinese characteristics

建设有中国特色社会主义的共同理想
the common ideals of building socialism with Chinese characteristics

建设有中国特色社会主义的经济[政治,文化]
build a socialist economy [politics, culture] with Chinese characteristics

建设有中国特色社会主义的新农村
build a new socialist countryside with Chinese characteristics

建筑业
construction industry; building industry

建筑材料业
building materials industry

健全社会主义法制
improve (or perfect) the socialist legal system

jiǎng

讲大局
stress the overall (or general) interests; stress the overall (or general) situation; take the overall interests (or situation) into account

讲党性,讲原则
stress Party spirit and principles

讲学习,讲政治,讲正气
stress the need to study, to be politically minded and to be honest and upright; stress (or give heed to) study, politics and healthy tendencies (or healthy trends)

奖学金
scholarship

jiāo

交通运输
communications and transportation

教书育人
impart knowledge and educate people

jiào

教师队伍
the ranks of teachers

教学(方)法
teaching method(s); method(s) of instruction

教学、科研、生产三结合
three-in-one combination of teaching, research and production

教学内容
content of courses; course content

教学质量
quality of instruction; quality of teaching

教育必须为社会主义现代化建设服务
Education must serve socialist modernization drive.

教育必须与生产劳动相结合
Education must be combined with productive labor.

教育方针
educational policy

教育改革和发展
reform and development of education

教育体制改革
reform of the educational structure (or system); reform of the

management system of education

教育质量
educational quality; quality of education

教育质量的评估和检查
assessment of and check-up for educational quality

教育资源
educational resources; resources for education

jié

节水[地,能,材,粮]
economize on (or save on) water [land, energy, materials, grain]

节水灌溉
water-saving irrigation

节水农业
an agriculture with good water-saving results; water-efficient agriculture

节约各种资源
economize on all the resources

节约能源与发展能源工业并重的方针
the principle of attaching equal importance to economizing on energy and the expansion of energy industry

jiě

解放生产力
emancipate (or liberate) the productive forces

解放思想
emancipate the mind

解放思想、实事求是的思想路线

ideological line of emancipating the mind and seeking truth from facts

解决温饱问题
solve the problem of food and clothing; provide adequate food and clothing

解决下岗职工的再就业问题
solve the problem of reemployment of the laid-off workers

jīn

金融（业）
finance; banking

金融风险
financial risks

金融机构
financial institution

金融机构体系
a system of financial institutions

金融市场（体系）
financial market（system）

金融体制改革
reform of the banking system

金融调控监管体系
financial control and supervision system

金融秩序
financial order

jìn

进出口结构
the import and export mix

进出口贸易
import and export trade; foreign trade; trade exchanges

jīng

经济布局
economic distribution

经济的社会化、市场化、现代化
the socialization, market orientation and modernization of the economy

经济发展速度
the rate of economic development

经济发展战略
economic development strategy

经济活力
economic vitality

经济基础
economic base

经济技术合作
economic and technological cooperation

经济技术开发区
economic and technological development zone

经济建设
economic development; economic construction

经济结构的战略性调整
strategic readjustment in the economic structure

经济结构调整
readjustment of (or in) the economic structure; structural readjustment in the economy

经济结构优化

optimization of the economic structure

经济全球化趋势
trend of economic globalization

《经济、社会、文化权利国际公约》
International Covenant on Economic, Social and Cultural Rights

经济特区
special economic zone

经济体制的根本转变
fundamental shift of the economic system

经济体制改革
reform of the economic structure; economic restructuring

经济效益
economic performance; economic returns (or results, or benefits)

经济协调发展
coordinated development of the economy

经济运行机制
economic operating mechanism; way of operating the economy

经济(稳定)增长
(stable) economic growth

经济增长方式从粗放型向集约型的转变
the shift from extensive mode to intensive mode in economic growth

经济增长方式的根本转变
fundamental shift of the mode of economic growth (or of the economic growth mode)

经济总量平衡
a balance between total demand and total supply

精简机构

streamlining organizations

精品意识
awareness of creating excellent works

精品战略
strategy of creating excellent works

精神产品
intellectual works

精神动力
ideological driving force

精神（文化）生活
cultural life

精神食粮
mental nourishment; nourishment for the mind

精神文明建设
cultural and ideological (or ethical) progress; ideological (or ethical) and cultural progress

精神支柱
ideological pillar (or prop); aspirations

jìng

竞技体育
competitive sports

竞技运动水平
the level of competitive sports

竞争机制
competitive mechanism

竞争力
competitive power; competitiveness

竞争主体

competitor; principal in competition

敬老院
house (or home) of respect for the aged; old folks' home

jiū

纠正不正之风
rectify unsound practices; correct unhealthy tendencies; correct mal-practices

jiǔ

九年义务教育
nine-year compulsory education

九三学社
Jiu San Society

jiù

就业服务体系
employment service system

就业服务中心
employment service center

就业培训中心
employment training center

jù

拒腐防变
guard against corruption and degeneration; resist corruption and guard against deterioration

jué

决策
decision-making; policy-decision(s); policy-making; make policy decision(s)

jūn

军地两用人才
personnel competent for both military and civilian services (or jobs)

军队建设
army building

军工技术的和平利用
peaceful uses for military industrial technologies

军工企业
military industrial enterprises

军控与裁军
arms control and disarmament

军民[警民]共建精神文明单位
build up civilized units with the joint efforts of the military and the civilians (or of the army and the people) [the police and the civilians (or the police and the people)]

军民结合
integrating the army with the people; the integration of the army with the people

军民团结
unity between (or of) the army and the people (or civilians)

军政团结
unity between (or of) the army and the government

军转民
transfer form military to civilian use in industrial technologies;
the transfer of military technology to civilian use

K

kāi

开发新产品［新技术］
develop new products ［new technologies］

开发优势资源
develop advantageous resources

开放城市
open city

开放型经济
an open economy

开放政策
the open policy

开拓进取
blaze new trails; make pioneering efforts; pioneer to make
progress; make bold exploration

开拓国内国外市场
open up (or explore) the domestic and foreign markets

开拓农村市场
open up (or explore) rural market

kāng

康复服务
rehabilitation service; convalescence service

康复中心
rehabilitation center; convalescence center

kàng

抗洪(斗争)
flood-fighting; fighting floods; the fight (or the battle, or the struggle) against floods; anti-flood battle

抗洪精神
the flood-fighting spirit

抗洪救灾(工作)
flood-fighting and disaster-relief work; fighting floods and providing disaster relief

抗洪抢险
fight floods and deal with emergencies; flood-fighting and emergency rescues

抗御自然灾害
resist (or fight) natural disasters

抗灾救灾
fight calamities and provide relief; fight disasters and provide disaster relief

kē

科技成果
scientific and technological achievements (or advances)

科技成果的商品化
commercialization of scientific and technological achievements

科技成果向现实生产力转化
the translation (or transformation) of scientific and technological achievements into practical (or actual, or real) productive forces

科技队伍
the contingent of scientific and technical personnel; the contingent of scientists and technicians; scientific and technical contingent

科技革命
scientific and technological revolution

科技攻关
tackling key problems in science and technology; the tackling of key scientific and technological problems

科技进步
scientific and technological progress (or advancement); progress in science and technology

科技强军
strengthen the army by relying on science and technology

科技人才
scientific and technical personnel; qualified scientists and technicians

科技水平
scientific and technological level

科技体制改革
reform of the management system of science and technology; reform of the system for managing science and technology

科教兴国战略
the strategy of developing the country by relying on science and education

科教兴农

develop agriculture by relying on science and education (or on science and technology and on education)

科学方法
scientific method(s)

科学管理
scientific management

科学技术的开拓者
pioneer in the development of science and technology

科学技术现代化
modernization of science and technology

科学精神
scientific spirit; scientific approach

科学社会主义
scientific socialism

科学实验
scientific experiment

科学、适度的消费模式
a scientific and moderate consumption pattern

科学文化素质
scientific and cultural quality (or levels)

科学研究
scientific research; research

科学种田
scientific farming

科研与开发(研究与开发)
research and development; R & D

科研院所
research academies and institutes

kě

可持续发展战略
the strategy of achieving sustainable development

kè

克己奉公
devote oneself to public duties wholeheartedly; be wholeheartedly devoted to public duties

kòng

控股
hold the controlling share

控股权
the controlling share

控制力
control power

控制农田污染和水污染
control pollution of farmland and water

控制人口数量
control the population size

控制人口增长
control the growth of population; control population growth

控制水土流失
control (water loss and) soil erosion

控制酸雨
control acid rain

kuà

跨地区的经济区域
cross-regional economic zone

跨地区的重点产业带
cross-regional key industrial belt

跨地区、跨行业、跨所有制和跨国经营的大企业集团
large enterprise groups with cross-regional, inter-trade, cross-ownership and transnational operations

跨国公司
transnational corporation

跨世纪发展宏伟目标
grand objectives for cross-century development

kuàng

矿产资源
mineral resources

kuò

扩大灌溉面积
enlarge irrigated area

扩大出口
increase exports; expand exports

扩大开放
open wider to the outside world

扩大内需
expand domestic demand

L

láo

劳动安全
labor safety; labor security

劳动保护
labor protection

劳动观点的教育
education in labor viewpoint

劳动合同制度
labor contract system

劳动技能的训练
training in labor skills

劳动监察制度
labor supervision system

劳动力市场［资源］
labor market［resources］

劳动密集型产业
labor-intensive industries

劳动生产率
labor productivity; productivity

劳动者的积极性和技术水平
the enthusiasm（or initiative）of the working people and the level of their technical skill

劳动者权益的保障

protection of the rights and interests of workers

劳动者素质
the quality of laborers

劳改(劳动改造)
reform (of criminals) through labor

劳改机关
reform-through-labor institution

lǎo

老干部
veteran cadre

老一辈无产阶级革命家
proletarian revolutionaries of the older generation

lǐ

理论联系实际
linking theory and (or with) practice; integrating theory with practice

lì

历史唯物主义
historical materialism

历史文化优秀传统
fine cultural traditions handed down from history; fine historical and cultural traditions

历史性的巨大变化
great historic change

历史性飞跃[决策]

historic leap [decision]

立法（工作）
legislation

立法质量
the quality of legislation

厉行节约
practice strict economy

利用国外资金[资源，技术，管理经验]
make use of foreign funds [resources, technology, management expertise]

利用外资
use (or utilize) foreign capital (or funds)

lián

联合国
the United Nations (UN)

联合国安全理事会
the United Nations Security Council (UNSC)

联合国安理会常任理事国
permanent member of the United Nations Security Council

联合国大会
the United Nations General Assembly

联合国宪章
the United Nations Charter

联合投资
joint investment

廉洁奉公
perform one's official duties honestly

廉洁自律

be honest, clean and self-disciplined

廉政建设
building an honest and clean government; the building of a
clean government

liáng

粮棉购销体制改革
reform of the grain and cotton purchasing and marketing system

粮棉稳定增产
steady increase of the output of grain and cotton; steadily increase the output of grain and cotton

粮食安全
grain security; stability of the grain market; food security

粮食储备制度
grain reserve system

粮食单位面积产量
per unit area yield of grain

粮食风险基金制度
grain risk fund system

粮食流通体制改革
reform of the grain circulation system (or distribution system)

粮食自给率
self-sufficiency rate of grain

粮食综合生产能力
the comprehensive grain production ability

粮食总产量
total grain output

liǎng

两岸关系
the relations between the two sides of the Taiwan Straits

两岸经济、科技、文化等领域的交流与合作
exchanges and cooperation between the two sides of the Taiwan Straits in various fields such as economy, science, technology and culture (or in economic, scientific, technological, cultural and other areas)

两岸人员往来
mutual visits of people between the two sides of the Taiwan Straits

两岸政治谈判
political negotiations between the two sides of the Taiwan Straits

两岸直接通邮、通航、通商
direct links of postal, air and shipping services and trade between the two sides of the Taiwan Straits

两个文明一起抓
pay equal attention to (or place equal emphasis on) material progress and cultural and ideological progress

两手抓,两手都要硬
do two types of work at the same tine, attaching equal importance to both; grasp two links at the same time and attach equal importance to both; work at two tasks and be steadfast with regard to both

lín

林业建设
construction in forestry; forestry development

林业生态工程
forest ecological project(s)

临海经济带和海洋经济区
coastal economic belts and marine economic zones

líng

灵活机动的战略战术
flexible strategy and tactics

lǐng

领导班子
leading body; leading group; the leadership

领导核心
leading core; the core of the leadership

领导集体
collective leadership

领导制度
the system of leadership

领海主权和毗连区管制权
sovereignty over the territorial seas and jurisdiction over the adjacent zones

领土、领空、领海主权
sovereignty over territorial land, air and seas

liú

流通领域
the field of circulation (or distribution)

流通体制改革

reform of the circulation（or distribution）system

lǚ

旅游业
tourism; the tourist industry

lǜ

绿化祖国
make our country green

绿色工程计划
green project

绿色[有机]食品
green [organic] food

M

mǎ

马克思列宁主义
Marxism-Leninism

马克思列宁主义[毛泽东思想，邓小平理论]的精髓
the quintessence of Marxism-Leninism [Mao Zedong Thought, Deng Xiaoping Theory]

马克思列宁主义同中国实际相结合

the integration of Marxism-Leninism with China's reality

马克思主义的立场、观点、方法
Marxist stand, viewpoint and method

马克思主义在中国发展的新阶段
a new stage of development of Marxism in China

máo

毛泽东思想
Mao Zedong Thought

毛泽东思想的继承和发展
continuation and development of Mao Zedong Thought

mào

贸易平衡
trade balance

贸易投资环境
trade and investment environment

贸易投资自由化
trade and investment liberalization

méi

煤炭工业
coal industry

měi

每周五天工作制
five-day work week

美育
aesthetic education; aesthetic culture

mǐ

"米袋子"工程
"rice bag" project

"米袋子"省长负责制
the system of provincial governors assuming responsibility for
the "rice bag"

mì

密切联系群众
forge close links with the masses; maintain close ties with the
masses

miàn

面向现代化,面向世界,面向未来
be geared to the needs of modernization, of the world and of
the future

mín

民兵、预备役部队
the militia and the reserves

民营企业
non-governmentally operated enterprise

民主参与
democratic participation

民主党派

democratic parties

民主的科学的决策制度
a system of democratic and scientific decision-making

民主法制观念
awareness of democracy and legality

民主法制建设
strengthening democracy and the legal system; the development
(or improvement) of democracy and the legal system; efforts
to develop democracy and improve the legal system

民主法制教育
education in democracy and legality (or the legal system)

民主管理
democratic management

民主集中制
democratic centralism

民主监督
democratic supervision

民主决策
democratic decision-making; making (policy) decisions in a
democratic manner

民主权利
democratic rights

民主讨论
democratic discussion

民主选举
democratic election

民主制度
system(s) of democracy

民族区域自治制度
the system of regional autonomy in areas inhabited by ethnic

minorities（or minority nationalities）; the system of regional autonomy of minority nationalities; regional national autonomy system; ethnic regional autonomy system

民族手工业
national handicrafts; traditional handicrafts; national handicraft industry

民族团结
the unity of the nationalities; national unity; ethnic unity

民族优秀文化传统
the fine traditions of national culture

民族振兴
rejuvenation of the（Chinese）nation

民族自尊、自信和自强精神
national spirit of self-respect, self-confidence and self-reliance（or self-improvement）

mǔ

母乳喂养工作
the work on breastfeeding

mù

睦邻友好关系
friendly and good-neighborly relations; good-neighborly relations

睦邻友好政策
good-neighborly policy

N

nài

耐用消费品
durable goods

nán

男女平等
equality of (or between) men and women

男女同工同酬原则
the principle of equal pay for equal work to men and women alike; the principle of men and women enjoying equal pay for equal work; the principle of equal remuneration for men and women for work of equal value

南极科学考察
scientific investigation in the Antarctic

南水北调工程
projects for diverting water from south to north

nèi

内陆中心城市
major cities in the hinterland

néng

能源工业
energy industry

níng

凝聚力
cohesion; cohesiveness

nóng

农产品价格体制改革
reform of the pricing system for agricultural products (or for farm produce)

农产品流通体制改革
reform of the circulation system for farm produce

农产品生产、加工、销售
the production, processing and marketing of farm produce

农产品市场体系
farm produce market system

农村产业结构
rural structure of production

农村改革
rural reform(s)

农村基层民主法制建设
strengthening democracy and the legal system at the rural grass-roots level

农村(集体)经济
rural (collective) economy

农村经济体制改革
rural reform of the economic structure; rural economic restructuring

农村居民人均纯收入
the average annual per-capita net income for rural residents

农村流通体制改革
reform of the rural circulation (or distribution) system

农村商业网点
a network of commercial establishments in rural areas; rural commercial establishments and networks

农村市场体系建设
the building of rural market system

农副产品加工业
farm and sideline product processing (industry)

农工贸一体化
the integration of agriculture, industry and trade

农林牧副渔各业
farming, forestry, animal husbandry, sideline production and fishery

农民的生产经营自主权
the decision-making power of peasants in their production and operations

农民的土地使用权
peasants' right to land-use

农民合法权益
the peasants' lawful rights and interests

农民合作经济组织
the peasants' cooperative economic organizations

农民收入
the peasants' income

农田基本建设
capital construction of farmland; construction of farmland improvement projects

农业产业化经营
industrial management of agriculture

农业持续稳定增长
sustained and steady growth of agriculture

农业多种经营
a diversified agricultural economy

农业机械化
mechanization of agriculture; farm mechanization

农业基础设施
agricultural infrastructure

农业集约经营
intensive management of agriculture

农业技术推广网络
agrotechnique popularization (or extension) network

农业抗灾能力
the ability of agriculture to withstand natural disasters

农业科技革命
scientific and technological revolution in agriculture

农业科技进步
scientific and technological progress in agriculture

农业科研、教育、推广相结合
integrate research, education and technique extension in agriculture

农业内部结构
agricultural structure

农业、农村、农民问题
the issues of agriculture, countryside and peasants; the issues of agriculture, rural areas and farmers

农业区域经济
regional economy in agriculture

农业商品化
commercialization of agriculture

农业社会化服务体系
socialized service system for agriculture

农业生产基础条件
the basic conditions for agricultural production

农业生产结构调整
readjustment of the structure of agricultural production

农业生产力水平
the level of agricultural productive forces; agricultural productivity

农业生产资料的生产和供应
the manufacture and supply of the means of agricultural production

农业生产资料流通体制改革
reform of the circulation (or distribution) system for the means of agricultural production

农业生态环境
ecological environment in (or for) agriculture

农业适度规模经营
agricultural production and operation at a proper scale; proper-scale operations of agriculture

农业投入
agricultural input; input (or investment) in agriculture

农业现代化
modernization of agriculture

农业专业化
specialization of agriculture

农业装备水平
the standards of agricultural equipment; the quality and quantity of farming equipment

农业综合开发
the overall development of agriculture

农业综合生产能力
overall productivity in agriculture

农业总产值
the total output value of agriculture

农用工业
agroindustry

P

pān

攀登现代科学技术高峰
scale the heights of modern science and technology

péi

培养和选拔妇女干部
foster and select women cadres

培养和选拔少数民族干部
foster and select cadres from among ethnic minorities (or cadres of ethnic minorities)

培养和选拔优秀年轻干部
train and select excellent young cadres

培养和造就社会主义事业的建设者和接班人
train and bring up builders of and successors to the cause of socialism

培育有理想、有道德、有文化、有纪律的公民
train people (or citizens) so that they have high ideals (or lofty ideals), moral integrity, a good education and a strong sense

of discipline

pèi

配套改革
supportive reforms; corresponding reforms

pī

批评与自我批评
criticism and self-criticism

píng

平等、民主、和睦的现代家庭关系
modern family mode marked by equality and a democratic and
harmonious atmosphere

平等、团结、互助的社会主义民族关系
socialist ethnic relations of equality, solidarity and mutual assistance; socialist relations of equality, unity and mutual assistance among the nationalities

平均预期寿命
average life expectancy

平原农田防护林网
a shelter-forest network for fields in the plains

平战结合
combining (or the combination of) peacetime with wartime

pǔ

普法教育
education of the populace about the law

普及环保知识
popularize environmental protection knowledge among the people

普及九年义务教育
make the nine-year compulsory education universal; popularization of compulsory nine-year schooling

普及科技知识
popularize science and technology

普通高等学校
regular institutions of higher learning

Q

qí

旗帜鲜明
take (or have) a clear-cut stand

qǐ

企业的改组[联合,兼并,租赁,承包经营,出售]
reorganization [association, merger, leasing, contract operation, sell-off] of enterprises

企业管理
business management; management of enterprises

企业环境监督管理
enterprise environment supervision and administration (or management)

企业集团
enterprise group

企业技术进步
technological progress of enterprise(s)

企业经营管理者队伍
the contingent of enterprise managers

企业经营机制
the way enterprises operate

企业决策[执行，监督]体系
the decision-making [enforcement, supervision] system of enterprise(s)

企业领导班子
the leadership of enterprise; the leading body of enterprise

企业领导体制
system of leadership in enterprises

企业市场竞争能力
competitiveness of enterprise(s) in the markets

企业文化
enterprise culture

企业运作效率
the efficiency of the operation of enterprise(s)

企业整体素质
the overall quality of enterprise(s)

企业组织管理制度
system of organization and management in enterprises

qiǎng

抢险救灾
deal with emergencies and disasters and provide relief; emergency rescues and disaster relief

qín

勤俭办一切事业
do everything through diligence and thrift

勤俭建国［建军］
build our country［army］through diligence and thrift

qīng

"青年志愿者"活动
"Young Volunteers" activity

青少年思想道德教育
education in ideology and ethics among the youth and young-sters（or among young people）

青壮年文盲率
the illiteracy rate of young and middle-aged people

轻纺工业
textile and other light industries

轻工业
light industry

清洁高效的工艺
clean and efficient technologies

清洁能源
clean energy

清洁生产
clean production

清正廉洁
be honest and clean; be upright and clean

qiú

求同存异
seek common ground while reserving differences; seek common ground while putting aside disagreements

求真务实
be realistic and pragmatic; seek truth and deal with concrete matters

qū

区域经济合作
regional economic cooperation

区域性、洲际性合作组织
regional and intercontinental organizations of cooperation

qǔ

取缔非法收入
ban illegal earnings; ban unlawful incomes; outlaw illicit incomes

quán

权利和义务
rights and duties

权责明确
well defined power and responsibility

全方位、多层次、宽领域的对外开放格局
the pattern of opening up in all directions, at all levels and in a wide range; an omni-directional, multi-level and wide-range

opening to the outside world

全国财政收入
national revenue

全国各族人民
the people of all nationalities in the country

《全国海洋开发规划》
National Program for Marine Development

全国劳动模范
national model worker

全国人大常委会委员长
Chairman of the Standing Committee of the National People's Congress

全国"三八"红旗手
national "March 8* Red-Banner Pacesetter"

《全国水土保持规划纲要》
National Program for Water and Soil Conservation

《全国土地利用总体规划纲要》
National Program for Overall Land Use Planning

全国"五一"劳动奖章
national "May 1" labor medal

《全国造林绿化规划纲要》
National Program for Afforestation

全海域海洋监测网
overall marine monitoring network

全局观念
awareness of the overall situation (or the overall interests)

全面改革
comprehensive reform; all-round reform

---

* March 8 means International Women's Day.

《全面禁止核试验条约》
Comprehensive Nuclear Test Ban Treaty

全面禁止和彻底销毁核武器和其他大规模杀伤性武器
complete prohibition and thorough destruction of nuclear weapons and other weapons of mass destruction

全面禁止和彻底销毁化学[生物]武器
complete prohibition and thorough destruction of chemical [biological] weapons

全面禁止和彻底销毁外空武器
complete prohibition and thorough destruction of outer space weapons

全面落实党和国家的各项政策
carry out (or implement) the policies of the Party and the state in an all-round way

全面提高教育质量
improve (or enhance) the overall quality of education

全面认识公有制经济的含义
see the full meaning of the public sector of the economy

全面质量管理
total quality management (TQM)

全民健身计划
physical fitness plan for the entire population

全民所有制
ownership by the whole people; ownership by the people as a whole

全民自卫原则
the principle of self-defense by the whole people

全球多边贸易体系
the global system of multilateral trade

全体社会主义劳动者
all socialist working people

全心全意为人民服务
serve the people wholeheartedly

全心全意依靠工人阶级
rely on the working class wholeheartedly

qún

群众监督
supervision by the masses

群众路线
the mass line

群众生活
the well-being of the masses

群众团体
mass organizations

群众性精神文明创建活动
mass activities to promote cultural and ideological progress

群众性文化[卫生，体育，科普]活动
mass activities on (or mass activities to promote) culture [health, sports, popular science]

R

rén

人才
competent people; talented person (s); qualified personnel; trained personnel; talent

人才流动
flow of trained personnel; flow of talent

人才培养[使用]
the training [use] of competent people

人才市场
talent market

人才资源开发
the exploitation of intellectual resources

人的全面发展
the overall (or all-round) development of human being

人均居住面积
per-capita housing; the average per-capita living area

人口控制
population control

人口出生率
birth rate; the birth rate for population

人口老龄化
aging of population; population aging; the growing population aging

人口平均预期寿命
the average life expectancy of the population

人口素质
the quality of population; population quality

人口自然增长率
natural growth rate of population; the rate of natural population increase; natural population growth rate

人类进步事业
the progress of mankind; the cause of human progress

人类灵魂工程师
engineer of the soul

人类文明
human civilization

人类文明的共同成果
common achievements of human civilization

人力资源开发
development of human resources

人民币不贬值的决策
the decision not to devalue the Renminbi

人民币经常项目下的可兑换
convertibility of the Renminbi under current accounts

人民代表大会制度
the people's congress system; the system of the people's congresses

人民当家作主的权利
the rights of the people as the masters of the country

人民的创造精神[积极性]
the creativeness [initiative] of the people

人民的利益
the interests of the people

人民的生存权和发展权
the people's rights to subsistence (or existence) and development; the people's rights to earn a living and develop

人民的信任[支持]
the confidence [support] of the people

人民法院
the people's court(s)

人民检察院
the people's procuratorate(s)

人民民主制度
the system of the people's democracy

人民民主专政
the people's democratic dictatorship

人民内部矛盾
contradictions among the people

人民生活水平
the people's living standards; the standard of living of the people

人民战争的战略思想
the strategic concept of the people's war

人民政协
the people's political consultative conference

人权
human rights

人权的普遍性原则与中国的具体国情相结合
combine the universality of human rights with China's real conditions

人权的司法保障
judicial guarantee for human rights

人权领域的国际交流与合作
international exchange and cooperation in the field of human rights

人人享有卫生保健
Everybody enjoys health care.

人生观
outlook on life

人事工作
personnel work

人事[劳动]制度改革
reform of the personnel [labor] system

人员流动

flow of personnel

rèn

认识世界，改造世界
understand the world and change it

认真学习
study conscientiously

任人唯贤
appoint people on their merits

róng

融资
financing

融资体制改革
reform of the financing system

ruǎn

软着陆
soft landing

S

sān

"三步走"发展战略
a three-step development strategy

"三个有利于"的标准
the criterion of "three favorables" *

三级医疗预防保健网
a three-level network of medical treatment, prevention and health care

三峡地区经济发展规划
the plan for economic development in Three Gorges area

"三资"企业
three kinds of foreign-invested ventures (i.e. the Chinese-foreign joint, the Chinese-foreign cooperative and foreign-owned); three kinds of foreign-funded enterprises (i.e. Chinese-foreign joint venture, Chinese-foreign contracted cooperation and exclusively foreign-funded enterprises)

sǎo

扫除黄赌毒等社会丑恶现象
eradicate social evils such as pornography, gambling and drug abuse and trafficking

扫除青壮年文盲
eliminate illiteracy among young and middle-aged people

"扫黄打非"
wipe out pornographic publications and crack down on illegal publishing practices; eliminate pornography and illegal publications

---

  * Deng Xiaoping Theory requires us to judge everything by the fundamental criterion whether it is favorable toward promoting the growth of the productive forces in a socialist society, increasing the overall strength of the socialist state and raising the people's living standards, or the "three favorables" for short.

sēn

森林保护
protection of the forests

森林资源的培育保护和管理
the fostering, protection and management of forest resources

shā

杀伤性地雷问题
the issue of anti-personnel landmines

shāng

商标国际注册
international registration of trademarks

商标注册
trademark registration

商标注册专用权
the right to exclusive use of a registered trademark

商品化
commercialization

商品贸易
trade in commodities

商品市场
commodity market

商业
commerce; business; trade

商业性金融

commercial banking

商业零售
retailing

商业银行
commercial bank

shàng

上层建筑
superstructure

上海浦东新区
the Pudong New Area in (or of) Shanghai

shǎo

少数民族
minority nationality; ethnic minority

shè

社会安定
social stability

社会保障体系
social security system

社会风气
social conduct; general social conduct; standards of social conduct; general mood of society

社会福利设施
social welfare facilities

社会福利事业
social welfare undertakings

社会福利院
social welfare institution

社会公德
social morality; public morality; social ethics

社会化生产
socialized production

社会救济制度
social relief system

社会科学
social sciences

社会全面进步
all-round social progress

社会生产力
（social）productive forces

社会统筹
overall social planning

社会统筹与个人帐户相结合的养老、医疗保险制度
old-age pensions and medical insurance systems combining social pools with individual accounts; old-age and medical insurance systems that combine overall social planning with personal
accounts

社会团体
social organizations

社会稳定
social stability

社会效益
social effect; social impact; social results; social benefits

社会需求
social demand

社会治安

public security; public order

社会治安综合管理
the improvement of all facets of public security

社会中介组织
social intermediary organizations

社会主义初级阶段
primary stage of socialism

社会主义道德
socialist ethics; socialist morality

社会主义道路
socialist road

社会主义的本质
the essence of socialism

社会主义的发展道路
the road to socialism

社会主义的发展动力
the motive force of socialist development

社会主义的发展阶段
the stages of development of socialism

社会主义的根本任务
the fundamental task of socialism

社会主义的依靠力量
forces to be relied on in building socialism

社会主义法治国家
socialist country ruled by law

社会主义法制
the socialist legal system

社会主义方向
socialist orientation; orientation of socialism

社会主义公有制
socialist public ownership

社会主义公有制为主体、多种所有制经济共同发展的基本经济制度
the basic economic system in which the socialist public ownership is dominant and different types (or diverse forms) of ownership develop side by side

社会主义基本制度
the basic system of socialism

社会主义建设
socialist construction

社会主义建设的外部条件
the external conditions for socialist construction

社会主义建设的战略步骤
the strategic steps for socialist construction

社会主义建设的政治保证
the political guarantee for socialist construction

社会主义精神文明建设
socialist cultural and ideological (or ethical) progress; socialist ideological (or ethical) and cultural progress

社会主义民主
socialist democracy

社会主义民主政治
socialist democracy; socialist democratic politics

社会主义民族关系
socialist relations among the nationalities

社会主义人道主义
socialist humanitarianism

社会主义市场经济(体制)
socialist market economy

社会主义市场经济法律体系
a legal system for socialist market economy

社会主义事业的建设者和接班人
builders of and successors to the cause of socialism

社会主义事业的领导核心
the force at the core leading the cause of socialism; the leading
core for the socialist cause

社会主义思想道德建设
socialist ideological and ethical progress

社会主义文化
socialist culture

社会主义文化建设
socialist cultural advancement; development of socialist culture

社会主义现代化
socialist modernization

社会主义现代化建设
socialist modernization drive

社会主义[共产主义,马克思主义]信念
socialist [communist, Marxist] conviction; faith (or belief) in
socialism [communism, Marxism]

社会主义制度优越性
the superiority of the socialist system

社会总资产
the total assets in society

社情民意
social conditions and popular feelings

社区服务
community services

社区康复服务
community rehabilitation (or convalescence) service

社区文化
community culture

涉外法律体系
foreign-related legal system

shēn

深海采矿
deep-sea mining

深化改革
deepen the reform

shěn

审计监督
supervision through auditing

shēng

生产关系
the relations of production; production relations

生产力
the productive forces

生产要素
(essential) factors of production; production factors; key elements of production

生产要素市场
markets for (essential) production factors

生产要素价格形成机制
the mechanism for pricing production factors

生活方式

way of life; lifestyle; life style

生活水平
living standards; standard of living

生活质量
the quality of life

生态环境保护[建设]
protection [improvement] of the ecological environment

生态农业建设
development (or construction) of eco-agriculture

生物多样性保护
bio-diversity conservation; protection of biological diversity

生物工程
bioengineering

生育保险
birth insurance

shī

失业保险
unemployment insurance

师范教育
teacher education; normal education

师资队伍
the ranks of teachers

师资训练
teacher training; normal training

湿地保护
protection of wetland

shí

石油工业
petroleum industry; oil industry

石油化工
petrochemical industry

石油及天然气
petroleum and natural gas; oil and gas

时代的要求[主流,主题]
the requirements [mainstream, themes] of the times

时代特征
the features of the times

实际投资额
paid-up investment volume

实践是检验真理的唯一标准
Practice is the sole criterion for testing truth.

实事求是
seek truth from facts

实现高技术产业化
apply high technology to production

实现外空"非武器化"
keep outer space "weapon free"

食品工业
food industry; foodstuffs industry

食品多样化生产
diversified food production

食品结构改革
dietary pattern reform

shì

市场供应
market supplies

市场管理
market management

市场规则
market rules

市场机制
market mechanism

市场价格调节
regulation by market price

市场竞争
market competition; competition for market(s)

市场竞争主体
market competitor(s); principal(s) in market competition

市场体系
market system

市场调节
regulation by market forces; market regulation

市场需求
demand(s) of the markets

市场中介组织
intermediary market organization

市场准入
market access

市政建设
municipal construction

世纪之交
the turn of the century

《世界版权公约》
Universal Copyright Convention

世界的多样性
the diversity of the world

世界多极化
global multi-polarization

世界观
world outlook

世界和平与发展
world peace and development

世界科技革命
scientific and technological revolution in the world

世界科技前沿
fields on the cutting edge of science and technology in the world; world frontier sciences and technologies

《世界人权宣言》
Universal Declaration of Human Rights

适度从紧的财政货币政策
appropriately tight (or stringent) financial and monetary policies

适度消费政策
policy of proper consumption

适龄儿童入学率
enrollment ratio for children of school age

shōu

收入分配
income distribution

shuǐ

水产资源保护
protection of the aquatic resources

水力发电
hydroelectric power generation; hydraulic power generation

水利建设
construction of water conservancy facilities (or of water-control facilities); the building of water conservancy projects; water conservancy construction

水土保持
water and soil conservation; soil retention

水[大气]污染防治
prevention and control of water [air] pollution

水资源的保护[合理开发, 可持续利用]
protection [rational development, sustainable use] of water resources

水资源的管理
the control over water resources

shuì

税收体制改革
reform of taxation (or the tax system)

税收征管
tax collection and management

shuò

硕士学位授予单位

unit granting master's degrees

硕士学位研究生
candidate for master's degree

sī

司法队伍
the ranks of judicial personnel

司法改革
the reform of judicial affairs

司法公正
judicial fairness

司法机关
judicial organ(s)

私营经济
private sector of the economy

私营企业
private enterprise; privately owned enterprise; private business

思想道德素质[修养]
ideological and ethical quality (or standards) [attainments]

思想上政治上同党中央保持一致
be in agreement with the Party Central Committee ideologically and politically

思想性和艺术性的统一
the integration of ideological content with artistry

思想政治工作
ideological and political work

sì

四个现代化

the Four Modernizations

四项基本原则
the Four Cardinal Principles

sù

素质教育
education for improving the quality of students; education with emphasis on improving the quality of students; quality-oriented education

suō

缩小地区经济发展差距
minimize the regional economic development disparities; narrow the regional gap(s) in economic development; narrow the gap(s) in economic development between different regions

suǒ

所有权和经营权分离
separation of ownership from management; separate ownership from management

所有者权益
the owner's equity

所有制结构
ownership structure

T

tái

台湾民主自治同盟
Taiwan Democratic Self-government League

台湾是中国不可分割的一部分
Taiwan is an inalienable part of China.

台湾同胞
compatriots in Taiwan; Taiwan compatriots

tè

特殊教育学校[班]
special education school [class]

tí

提高党的领导水平和执政水平
improve the Party's leading and governing ability; make the Party exercise more effective leadership and power

提高对外开放水平
do better in opening to the outside world

提高国民经济整体素质和效益
improve the quality and performance of the entire national economy; improve the overall quality and performance of the national economy

提高环境质量
improve the quality of environment

提高科技进步对经济增长的贡献率
increase the contribution of scientific and technological progress to economic growth

提高马克思主义的理论水平
acquire a better understanding of the theory of Marxism; raise the level of one's understanding of Marxist theory

提高能源利用效率
raise the energy utilization efficiency

提高农业装备水平
improve the standard of agricultural equipment

提高全民族的思想道德素质和教育科学文化水平
raise the ideological and ethical standards and the educational, scientific and cultural levels of the whole nation

提高人口素质
improve the population quality

提高人民生活水平
raise the people's living standards; raise the standard of living of the people

提高人民生活质量
improve the quality of the people's life

提高森林植被覆盖率
increase the coverage rate of forests (or forest vegetation)

提高土地使用效率
raise the land utilization efficiency

提高资源利用效率
raise the efficiency of utilizing natural resources

tǐ

体育
physical education; physical culture; sports

体育道德
sports ethics; sportsmanship

体育事业的改革和发展
the reform and development of sports

体育运动
physical culture and sports

tiáo

调节过高收入
regulate the excessively high incomes

调控力度
the degree of the control

调整产品结构
readjust the product mix (or the mix of products)

调整和完善所有制结构
readjust and improve the ownership structure

调整和优化产业结构
readjust and optimize the industrial structure (or the structure of production)

调整和优化经济结构
readjust and optimize the economic structure

调整能源结构
readjust the energy structure

调整企业组织结构
readjust the organizational structure of enterprises

tóng

同党中央保持一致
be in agreement with the Party Central Committee

同心同德
with one heart and one mind; be of one heart and one mind

tǒng

统分结合的双层经营体制
two-tier operation system that combines unified management with independent (or separate) management; two-tier management system that combines unification and diversification (or separation)

统一的多民族国家
a unitary multi-national state

统一开放、竞争有序的市场体系
a unified and open market system with orderly competition

统一战线
united front

tóu

投入与产出
input and output

投资体制改革
reform of the investment system

投融资体制改革
reform of investment and financing systems

投资主体
major investor; principal for investment

tǔ

土地保护[开发,整治]
land preservation [exploitation, control]

土地承包关系
land contract relations

土地承包期
land contract period (or term)

土地承包期再延长 30 年的政策
the policy of prolonging (or extending) the land contract period
(or term) for another 30 years

土地管理
land administration

土地开发复垦
land development and reclamation

土地利用综合规划
overall land use planning; overall plan for land use

土地市场
land market

土地适度规模经营
proper-scale land operation; operation of land at a proper scale

tuán

团结稳定的社会政治局面
social and political unity and stability

团结一切可以团结的力量
unite with all the forces that can be united

团结、友爱、互助的社会风尚
the social virtues (or practices) of unity, friendship and mutual
assistance

tuō

脱贫致富

shake off poverty and become prosperous; get rid of poverty and become well-off

W

wài

外国对华服务贸易
foreign service exports to China

外国文化有益成果
advances of foreign culture

外汇体制改革
reform of the foreign exchange system

外贸企业
foreign trade enterprise

外贸体制改革
reform of the foreign trade system

外向型经济
export-oriented economy

外商对华投资
foreign investment in China

外商投资企业
foreign-funded enterprise; foreign-invested enterprise

wǎn

晚婚晚育
marry late and have children late; delayed marriage and de-

layed child bearing

wēi

微电子技术
microelectronic technology

wéi

唯物辩证的思想方法和工作方法
materialist dialectical methods of thinking and work

唯物辩证法
materialist dialectics

维护大局
safeguard (or protect) overall interests

维护党的团结和统一
safeguard the unity and unification of the Party

维护法律尊严
safeguard the dignity (or sanctity) of the law

维护国际和平、安全和稳定
safeguard international peace, security and stability

维护国家安全［统一］
safeguard national security [unification]; safeguard the security [unification] of the country

维护国家的主权和领土完整
safeguard the sovereignty and territorial integrity of the country

维护国家和人民的利益
safeguard the interests of the state and the people

维护国家经济安全
safeguard the economic security of the country

维护海洋健康
maintain the wholesomeness of the oceans

维护民族团结
safeguard the unity of the nationalities

维护社会稳定
safeguard social stability

维护世界和平
safeguard world peace

维护宪法尊严
safeguard the dignity（or sanctity）of the Constitution

维护中央的权威
safeguard the authority of the central leadership

wèi

卫生管理体制改革
reform of the public health management system; reform of the
management system of public health

卫生事业的改革和发展
the reform and development of public health

卫生事业同经济社会的协调发展
a coordinated development between public health and the economy and society

卫星传输
satellite transmission

卫星地面接收站
ground satellite（receiving）station

卫星发射
satellite launching

卫星气象系统
the meteorological satellite system

卫星通信
satellite telecommunications

卫星遥感技术
satellite remote sensing technology

为群众办实事、办好事
do practical things in the interests of the masses

为人民服务、为社会主义服务的方向
the orientation (or principle) of serving the people and (the cause of) socialism

为人民健康服务
serve the people's health

为社会主义现代化建设服务
serve the socialist modernization drive

未成年人保护
protection of minors (or juveniles)

wēn

温饱
have adequate food and clothing

wén

文化环境
cultural environment

文化建设
cultural advancement

文化经济政策
economic policies concerning (or relating to) cultural undertakings

文化科技卫生下乡活动
activities to bring culture, science and technology, and medical
and health care to the countryside

文化(基础)设施
cultural establishments

文化市场
cultural market; markets for cultural products

文化事业
cultural undertakings

文化体制改革
reform of the system for managing cultural undertakings

文化遗产
cultural heritage

文明城市
civilized city

文明村镇
civilized villages and townships

文明单位
civilized unit

文明服务示范"窗口"
exemplary "window(s)" offering civilized service

文明家庭
civilized household

文明企业[事业单位]
civilized enterprise [institution]

文明科学进步的生活方式
civilized, scientific and progressive life style

文学和艺术作品
literary and artistic works

文学艺术

literature and art

文艺创作
literary and artistic creation

文艺工作者
writers and artists; literary and art workers

文艺评论
comments on literature and art; literary or art criticism

wěn

稳定的社会秩序[政治环境]
stable public order [political environment]

稳定压倒一切
Stability overrides everything else.

稳中求进
seek progress amid stability; seek further progress on the basis
of stability; seek further progress under stable conditions

wū

污染防治
pollution prevention and control

污染物排放标准
pollutant discharge or emission standards

污染限期治理
setting deadlines for eliminating pollution

wú

无产阶级革命家
proletarian revolutionary

无产阶级专政
dictatorship of the proletariat; proletarian dictatorship

wǔ

五年计划
five-year plan (e.g. three five-year plans); Five-Year Plan
(e.g. the Ninth Five-Year Plan)

武器装备现代化
modernization of weaponry

wù

物业管理
property management

物质生活
material well-being; material life

物质文明
material civilization

物质文明建设
material progress

X

xī

西藏是中国不可分割的一部分
Tibet is an inalienable part of China.

吸收人类文明发展的优秀成果
assimilate the outstanding achievements of the development of human civilization

吸收和借鉴世界各国的先进技术和管理经验
absorb and use for reference the advanced technology and managerial expertise of other countries

吸收外商投资
attract foreign investment

"希望工程"
Hope Project

xià

下岗分流
divert laid-off workers

下岗职工
laid-off workers

xiān

先进集体[个人]
advanced group [individual]

先进经验[水平]
advanced experience [level]

先进科学技术
advanced science and technology

先进生产[工作]者
advanced producer [worker]

先进适用技术
advanced and applicable techniques

先进思想的传播者

propagator of advanced thoughts

xiàn

宪法和法律
Constitution and laws; Constitution and other laws

现代服务业
modern service industry

现代工业［农业，国防，科学技术］
modern industry［agriculture, national defense, science and technology］

现代化正规化的革命军队
modernized and regularized (or standardized) revolutionary army

现代技术特别是高技术条件下的防卫作战能力
defense capabilities under modern technology and especially high-tech conditions

现代金融体系
modern financial system

现代企业制度
modern enterprise system

xiāng

乡镇企业
township enterprises; town and township enterprises; township and village enterprises

香港回归祖国
Hong Kong's return to the motherland

香港特别行政区
the Hong Kong Special Administrative Region (HKSAR)

香港特别行政区政府[行政长官]
the government [Chief Executive] of the HKSAR; HKSAR
government [Chief Executive]

香港自由港[国际金融、贸易、航运中心]地位
Hong Kong's status of a free port [an international financial,
trade and shipping center]

xiǎng

享受政府特殊津贴的专家、学者
specialists and scholars who enjoy special government allowances

xiāo

消除两极分化
eliminate polarization

消费品零售总额
the total retail sales volume of consumer goods

消费品市场
consumer goods market

消费者权益
the rights and interests of consumers

消灭剥削
eliminate exploitation

xiǎo

小城镇建设
construction of small towns and cities (or small towns)

小康(生活)
a fairly (or relatively) comfortable life

xiào

效率优先,兼顾公平
give priority to efficiency with due consideration to equity

校园文化
campus culture

xié

协议投资额
committed investment volume

xīn

新的经济增长点
new point (s) of (or for) economic growth; new economic growth point (or area)

新技术革命
new technological revolution

新能源[新材料]的研究开发
research and development of new sources of energy [new materials]

新闻出版(事业)
the press and publishing

新闻媒体
news media

新闻宣传
publicity through the press

新生儿计划免疫率
the rate of planned immunity for new-born babies

新兴产业
rising industries; burgeoning industries

新兴带头学科
rising and leading disciplines

xìn

信息产业
information industry

信息处理现代化
modernization of information processing

信息高速公路
information superhighway

信息技术
information technology

信用合作社
credit cooperative

xīng

兴修水利
engage in water conservancy projects

"星火计划"
Spark Program

xíng

行政复议
administrative reconsideration

行政管理权
administrative power; executive power

行政管理体制改革
reform of the administrative system

行政监察机关
organs supervising government administration

行政执法部门
administrative law-enforcement departments

xìng

"幸福工程"
Happiness Project*

xuān

宣传工作
publicity work; propaganda work

宣传舆论工作
publicity (or propaganda) work and guidance for public opinion

xué

学前教育
preschool education

学位制度
academic degree system

学习法律［管理,经济学,现代科学技术知识］
study law［management, economics, modern science and technology］

---

* This project is designed to help poverty-stricken mothers.

学习历史
study history

学习马列主义、毛泽东思想特别是邓小平理论的新高潮
a new upsurge in studying Marxism-Leninism, Mao Zedong
Thought and particularly Deng Xiaoping Theory

学习社会主义市场经济知识
study socialist market economy know-how; study the knowledge of socialist market economy

学习中国近代史、现代史、中共党史
study the history of modern and contemporary China and the
history of the Communist Party of China

学校的德育[智育，体育，美育]
moral education [intellectual education, physical education,
aesthetic education] in schools

学校内部管理体制改革
reform of the internal management system of the schools

学以致用
study for the sake of application

Y

yà

亚太地区
Asia-Pacific region

亚太经合组织
Asia-Pacific Economic Cooperation（APEC）

亚太经合组织中国企业联席会议
China APEC Enterprises Assembly

亚洲金融危机
financial crisis in Asia; Asian financial crisis

亚洲运动会
Asian Games

yán

严格管制敏感材料、技术与军事装备的转让
strictly control transfer of sensitive materials, technologies and military equipment

严格控制新开工项目
strictly control the launching of new projects

严格遵守[执行]党的纪律
strictly observe [enforce] Party discipline

严格遵守[执行]宪法和法律
strictly abide by [enforce] the Constitution and laws (or Constitution and other laws)

严禁各种形式的乱摊派、乱收费、乱罚款
strictly ban all kinds of arbitrary quotas, charges and fines

严厉打击各种犯罪活动
severely crack down on all kinds of crime (or on various criminal activities)

沿边地区
the areas along the borders

沿海地区
coastal areas

沿海经济开放区
open coastal economic development areas

沿海开放城市
open coastal city (or cities)

沿海陆地区域和海洋区域一体化开发
exploiting the coastal land and sea areas in a unified way

沿(长)江城市
city (or cities) along the Yangtze River

沿交通干线地区
the areas along main communications lines

研究生培养制度
system of training graduate students

研究新情况，解决新问题
study (or examine) new situations and solve (or tackle) new problems

yǎng

养老保险
old-age insurance

养老保险制度
the old-age insurance system; the old-age pensions system; insurance system for the aged

yī

一个国家,两种制度("一国两制")
one country, two systems

一个中国的原则
the principle that there is only (or but) one China; the principle of one China

一个中心,两个基本点
one central task, two basic points

一切从社会主义初级阶段的实际出发
proceed in everything we do from the realities (or the actual

situation) of the primary stage of socialism

一切从实际出发
proceed from reality in everything we do; proceed in all cases from reality

一切为了群众
serve the interests of the masses in everything we do; everything for the masses

一切相信[依靠]群众
have faith in [rely on] the masses in everything we do; faith in [reliance on] the masses in everything

医疗保健
medical and health care

医疗保险
medical insurance

医疗卫生事业
medical and health services

依法行使权力
exercise one's authority within the framework of law; exercise power according to law

依法治国
manage state affairs according to law; administer (or govern) the country according to law; rule the country by law

依靠各族人民的团结
rely on the unity of the people of all nationalities

依靠工人、农民、知识分子
rely on workers, peasants and intellectuals

yí

遗传工程
genetic engineering

yǐ

以经济建设为中心
take economic development as the central task; make economic development the central task; center on (or focus on) economic development

以科学的理论武装人
以正确的舆论引导人
以高尚的精神塑造人
以优秀的作品鼓舞人
arm people's minds with scientific theory
guide people in correct public opinion
mould people with noble spirit
inspire people with excellent (literary and artistic) works

以质取胜和市场多元化战略
strategy of achieving success on the strength of quality (or strategy of success through quality) and a multi-outlet market

yì

意识形态领域
ideological sphere

抑制通货膨胀
curtail (or curb, or control) inflation

义务教育和职业教育相结合
combine compulsory education with vocational education

yǐn

引进国外智力
bring in intellectual resources from overseas; introduce foreign intelligence; recruit overseas intelligence

引进先进技术［关键设备，管理经验］
introduce (or import) advanced technology (or technologies) [key equipment, managerial expertise]

yīng

应用技术
applied technologies

应用科学
applied sciences

yōng

拥护社会主义的爱国者
patriots who support socialism

拥护祖国统一的爱国者
patriots who stand for (or support) the reunification of the motherland

拥军优属
support the army and give preferential treatment to families of armymen (or servicemen) and martyrs

拥政爱民
support the government and cherish the people

yòng

用邓小平理论教育干部和群众
educate cadres and the masses in Deng Xiaoping Theory

用邓小平理论武装全党
arm the whole Party with Deng Xiaoping Theory

yōu

优化产业结构
optimize the structure of production

优化教育结构
optimize the educational structure

优化经济[资本]结构
optimize the economic [capital] structure

优化人口结构
optimize the population structure

优化膳食模式
optimize dietary scheme

优生优育
prenatal and postnatal care; bear and rear better children

优胜劣汰的竞争机制
a competitive mechanism for selecting the superior and eliminating the inferior

优势产业
superior industry; strong industry

优势互补
take advantage of each other's strengths

优秀精神产品的生产者
producer(s) of excellent intellectual works

优质服务
top quality service

yóu

邮电

post and telecommunications

yǒu

有法可依,有法必依,执法必严,违法必究
There must be laws to go by, the laws must be observed and strictly enforced, and law-breakers must be prosecuted.

有理想、有道德、有文化、有纪律的公民
people (or citizens) who have high ideals, moral integrity, a good education and a strong sense of discipline

有中国特色的社会主义
socialism with Chinese characteristics

yòu

又红又专
both red and expert; both politically conscious and professionally competent

又有集中又有民主,又有纪律又有自由,又有统一意志、又有个人心情舒畅、生动活泼的政治局面
a political situation in which we have both centralism and democracy, both discipline and freedom, both unity of will and personal ease of mind and liveliness

幼儿教育
infant school education; preschool education

yú

舆论导向
orientation of public opinion; guidance of public opinion

舆论监督
supervision by public opinion

yù

育龄群众
people of child-bearing age

育龄群众生殖保健
the reproductive health care for people of child-bearing age

yuán

原材料工业
raw and processed (or semi-finished) materials industries

yuǎn

远程教育
long-distance education

远大理想
lofty ideals

远景目标
long-range objectives

yǔn

允许一部分地区一部分人先富起来
allow some areas and some people to become prosperous (or grow rich, or get wealthy) first

yuàn

院士

academician

Z

zài

再就业服务中心
re-employment service center

再就业工程
re-employment project

zào

噪声污染防治
The prevention and control of noise pollution

造船业
shipbuilding industry

zé

责任与风险共担
sharing responsibilities and risks

zhé

哲学社会科学
philosophy and (other) social sciences

zhèn

振兴中华
rejuvenate China; revitalize the Chinese nation

zhěng

整顿经济秩序
rectify the economic order

zhèng

正确处理人民内部矛盾
correctly handle contradictions among the people

正确的世界观、人生观、价值观
correct outlook(s) on the world and life and correct values;
correct world outlook, outlook on life and values

证券市场
securities market

政策性金融[银行]
non-commercial banking [bank]; policy-related banking
[bank]

政法队伍
the ranks of procuratorial, judicial and public security personnel

政法工作
procuratorial, judicial and public security work

政风
the work style of the government; government conduct

政府机构改革

reform of the structure of government institutions; reform of the organizational structure of the government; reform of the government structure; institutional restructuring of the government

政企分开
separate the functions of the government from those of enterprises; separate government functions from enterprise management; separation of administrative functions from enterprise management; separation of enterprise from administration

政协全国委员会主席
Chairman of the CPPCC National Committee

政治合格、军事过硬、作风优良、纪律严明、保障有力的 (军队建设)总要求
the general requirements (with regard to army building) of being qualified politically and competent militarily and having a fine style of work, strict discipline and adequate logistical support

政治经济学
political economy

政治谈判
political negotiations

政治体制改革
reform of the political structure; political restructuring

政治协商
political consultation

zhī

支柱产业
pillar industries

知识产权
intellectual property rights (IPR)

知识产权保护制度
intellectual property rights protection system

知识产权法律制度
the legal system for the protection of intellectual property rights

知识产权审判庭
intellectual property rights court

知识产权意识
awareness（or understanding）of intellectual property rights

知识创新
knowledge innovation

知识分子是工人阶级的一部分
Intellectuals are part of the working class.

知识分子同工农群众相结合
the integration of the intellectuals with the masses of workers and peasants

知识经济
knowledge economy

zhí

执法队伍
the ranks of law-enforcing personnel

执法监督
supervision over law enforcement

执法监督部门
departments supervising law enforcement

执法检查
inspection of law enforcement

执法体系
law enforcement system

执法责任制
a system of responsibility for law enforcement

执政党
the party in power; the ruling party; the governing party

直接融资
direct financing

职工代表大会
workers' conference; congress of workers and (office) staff

职业道德
occupational ethics; professional ethics

职业技能
job skill

职业(技术)教育
vocational (and technical) education

职业介绍机构
employment agency

职业培训
job training; professional training ; vocational training

职业中学
vocational secondary school

植树造林
afforestation; afforest

植树种草
plant trees and grass

zhì

治理大江大河大湖
harness large rivers and lakes

治理污染的设施

pollution treatment facilities

志愿者助残行动
volunteers helping the disabled activities

智力劳动成果
fruits of mental labor

智力支持
intellectual support

智育
intellectual education; intellectual culture

质量管理
quality management

质量检验
quality inspection

质量控制
quality control

质量体系认证
quality system certification

zhōng

中等发达国家水平
the level of the moderately developed countries

中等技术学校
secondary technical school

中等教育
secondary (school) education

中等师范学校
secondary teacher-training school; secondary normal school

中等学校
secondary school

中等专业学校
specialized secondary school

中共中央（中国共产党中央委员会）
the Central Committee of the Communist Party of China; the
Central Committee of the CPC; the CPC Central Committee

中共中央政治局
the Political Bureau of the CPC Central Committee

中共中央政治局常务委员会
the Standing Committee of the Political Bureau of the CPC
Central Committee

中共中央总书记
General Secretary of the Central Committee of the CPC

中国奥林匹克委员会
the Chinese Olympic Committee

中国残疾人联合会
China Disabled Persons' Federation

中国道教协会
Taoist Association of China

《中国二十一世纪议程——中国二十一世纪人口、环境与
发展白皮书》
China's Agenda 21—White Paper on China's Population, Environment and Development in the 21st Century

中国佛教协会
Buddhist Association of China

《中国妇女发展纲要》
Program for the Chinese Women's Development

中国工程院
the Chinese Academy of Engineering

中国共产党
the Communist Party of China (CPC); the Chinese Communist
Party

中国共产党的领导
the leadership of (or by) the Communist Party of China

中国共产党全国代表大会
the National Congress of the Communist Party of China

中国共产党十一届三中全会
the Third Plenary Session of the 11th Central Committee of the CPC

中国共产党章程
Constitution of the Communist Party of China

中国共产党中央纪律检查委员会
the Central Commission for Discipline Inspection of the Communist Party of China

中国共产主义青年团
the Communist Youth League of China

中国国民党革命委员会
China Revolutionary Committee of the Kuomintang

《中国海洋二十一世纪议程》
China Ocean Agenda 21

中国基督教三自(自治、自养、自传)爱国运动委员会
Three-Selfs (i.e. self-administration, self-support and self-propagation) Patriotic Movement Committee of the Protestant Churches of China

中国基督教协会
China Christian Council

《中国教育改革和发展纲要》
China's Program for the Reform and Development of Education

中国科学技术协会(中国科协)
the Chinese Science and Technology Association

中国科学院
the Chinese Academy of Sciences

中国民主促进会
China Association for Promoting Democracy

中国民主建国会
China Democratic National Construction Association

中国民主同盟
China Democratic League

中国农工民主党
Chinese Peasants' and Workers' Democratic Party

《中国七大江河流域综合规划》
Comprehensive Plan for China's Seven Major River Valleys

中国人民对外友好协会
the Chinese People's Association for Friendship with Foreign Countries

中国人民解放军
the Chinese People's Liberation Army（the Chinese PLA）

中国人民解放军驻香港部队
the Chinese PLA Hong Kong Garrison

中国人民外交学会
the Chinese People's Institute of Foreign Affairs

中国人民武装警察部队
the Chinese People's Armed Police

中国人民政治协商会议
the Chinese People's Political Consultative Conference （CPPCC）

中国人民政治协商会议全国委员会(政协全国委员会)
the National Committee of the CPPCC; the CPPCC National Committee

中国少年先锋队
China Young Pioneers

中国社会科学院

the Chinese Academy of Social Sciences

中国天主教爱国会
Chinese Patriotic Catholic Association

中国天主教主教团
Chinese Catholic Bishops' College

中国文学艺术界联合会
China Federation of Literary and Art Circles

中国亚太经合组织科技产业合作基金
China APEC Science and Technology Industry Cooperation
Fund

中国伊斯兰教协会
Islamic Association of China

中国致公党
China Zhi Gong Dang

中华民族伟大复兴
a great rejuvenation of the Chinese nation

中华全国妇女联合会
All-China Women's Federation

中华全国工商业联合会
All-China Association (or Federation) of Industry and Commerce

中华全国归国华侨联合会
All-China Federation of Returned Overseas Chinese

中华全国青年联合会
All-China Youth Federation

中华全国学生联合会
All-China Students' Federation

中华全国总工会
All-China Federation of Trade Unions

中华人民共和国

the People's Republic of China（PRC）

《中华人民共和国澳门特别行政区基本法》
Basic Law of the Macao Special Administrative Region of the People's Republic of China

《中华人民共和国保守国家秘密法》
Law of the People's Republic of China on Guarding State Secrets

《中华人民共和国保险法》
Insurance Law of the People's Republic of China

《中华人民共和国标准化法》
Standardization Law of the People's Republic of China

《中华人民共和国兵役法》
Military Service Law of the People's Republic of China

《中华人民共和国残疾人保障法》
Law of the People's Republic of China on the Protection of Disabled Persons

《中华人民共和国草原法》
Grassland Law of the People's Republic of China

《中华人民共和国测绘法》
Survey-Cartography Law of the People's Republic of China

《中华人民共和国产品质量法》
Law of the People's Republic of China on Product Quality

《中华人民共和国城市房地产管理法》
Law of the People's Republic of China on the Management of Urban Real Estate

《中华人民共和国城市规划法》
City Planning Law of the People's Republic of China

《中华人民共和国城市居民委员会组织法》
Organic Law of the Urban Residents' Committees of the People's Republic of China

《中华人民共和国传染病防治法》
Law of the People's Republic of China on the Prevention and Control of Infectious Diseases

《中华人民共和国促进科技成果转化法》
Law of the People's Republic of China on Promoting the Transformation of Scientific and Technological Achievements into Productive Forces

《中华人民共和国村民委员会组织法》
Organic Law of the Villagers' Committees of the People' Republic of China

《中华人民共和国大气污染防治法》
Law of the People's Republic of China on the Prevention and Control of Air Pollution

《中华人民共和国担保法》
Guaranty Law of the People's Republic of China

《中华人民共和国档案法》
Archives Law of the People's Republic of China

《中华人民共和国地方各级人民代表大会和地方各级人民政府组织法》
Organic Law of the Local People's Congresses and Local People's Governments at Various Levels of the People's Republic of China

《中华人民共和国缔结条约程序法》
Procedural Law of the People's Republic of China on Concluding Treaties

《中华人民共和国电力法》
Electricity Law of the People's Republic of China

《中华人民共和国动物防疫法》
Law of the People's Republic of China on Epidemic Prevention for Animals

《中华人民共和国对外贸易法》
Foreign Trade Law of the People's Republic of China

《中华人民共和国法官法》
Judges Law of the People's Republic of China

《中华人民共和国反不正当竞争法》
Law of the People's Republic of China on Combating Unfair Competition

《中华人民共和国防洪法》
Flood Prevention Law of the People's Republic of China

《中华人民共和国防震减灾法》
Law of the People's Republic of China on Taking Precautions Against Earthquakes and Reducing Disasters

《中华人民共和国妇女权益保障法》
Law of the People's Republic of China on the Protection of Women's Rights and Interests

《中华人民共和国高等教育法》
Law of the People's Republic of China on Higher Education

《中华人民共和国个人所得税法》
Individual Income Tax Law of the People's Republic of China

《中华人民共和国工会法》
Law of the People's Republic of China on Trade Unions

《中华人民共和国公路法》
Law of the People's Republic of China on Highways

《中华人民共和国公民出境入境管理法》
Law of the People's Republic of China on the Control of Exit and Entry of Citizens

《中华人民共和国公司法》
Corporation Law of the People's Republic of China

《中华人民共和国固体废物污染环境防治法》
Law of the People's Republic of China on the Prevention and Control of Environmental Pollution by Solid Wastes

《中华人民共和国广告法》
Advertisement Law of the People's Republic of China

《中华人民共和国归侨侨眷权益保护法》
Law of the People's Republic of China on the Protection of the Rights and Interests of Returned Overseas Chinese and of the Family Members of Overseas Chinese

《中华人民共和国国防法》
National Defense Law of the People's Republic of China

《中华人民共和国国徽法》
Law of the People's Republic of China on the National Emblem

《中华人民共和国国籍法》
Nationality Law of the People's Republic of China

《中华人民共和国国家安全法》
State Security Law of the People's Republic of China

《中华人民共和国国家赔偿法》
State Compensation Law of the People's Republic of China

《中华人民共和国国境卫生检疫法》
Frontier Health and Quarantine Law of the People's Republic of China

《中华人民共和国国旗法》
Law of the People's Republic of China on the National Flag

中华人民共和国国务院
the State Council of the People's Republic of China

《中华人民共和国国务院组织法》
Organic Law of the State Council of the People's Republic of China

《中华人民共和国海关法》
Customs Law of the People's Republic of China

《中华人民共和国海商法》
Maritime Law of the People's Republic of China

《中华人民共和国海上交通安全法》
Maritime Traffic Safety Law of the People's Republic of China

《中华人民共和国海洋环境保护法》
Marine Environmental Protection Law of the People's Republic of China

《中华人民共和国合伙企业法》
Law of the People's Republic of China on Enterprises in Partnership

《中华人民共和国合同法》
Contract Law of the People's Republic of China

《中华人民共和国红十字会法》
Law of the People's Republic of China on the Red Cross

《中华人民共和国环境保护法》
Environmental Protection Law of the People's Republic of China

《中华人民共和国环境噪声污染防治法》
Law of the People's Republic of China on the Prevention and Control of Pollution by Environmental Noise

《中华人民共和国婚姻法》
Marriage Law of the People's Republic of China

《中华人民共和国集会游行示威法》
Law of the People's Republic of China on Assembly, Procession and Demonstration

《中华人民共和国计量法》
Metrology Law of the People's Republic of China

《中华人民共和国技术合同法》
Technology Contract Law of the People's Republic of China

《中华人民共和国继承法》
Inheritance Law of the People's Republic of China

《中华人民共和国价格法》
Price Law of the People's Republic of China

《中华人民共和国监狱法》
Prison Law of the People's Republic of China

《中华人民共和国检察官法》
Public Procurators Law of the People's Republic of China

《中华人民共和国建筑法》
Construction Law of the People's Republic of China

《中华人民共和国教师法》
Teachers Law of the People's Republic of China

《中华人民共和国教育法》
Education Law of the People's Republic of China

《中华人民共和国节约能源法》
Law of the People's Republic of China on Economy of the Sources of Energy

《中华人民共和国戒严法》
Martial Law of the People's Republic of China

《中华人民共和国进出境动植物检疫法》
Law of the People's Republic of China on Entry and Exit Quarantine of Animals and Plants

《中华人民共和国进出口商品检验法》
Law of the People's Republic of China on Import and Export Commodity Inspection

《中华人民共和国经济合同法》
Economic Contract Law of the People's Republic of China

《中华人民共和国军事设施保护法》
Law of the People's Republic of China on the Protection of Military Facilities

《中华人民共和国科学技术进步法》
Law of the People's Republic of China on Scientific and Technological Progress

《中华人民共和国会计法》
Accounting Law of the People's Republic of China

《中华人民共和国矿产资源法》
Mineral Resources Law of the People's Republic of China

《中华人民共和国矿山安全法》
Mine Safety Law of the People's Republic of China

《中华人民共和国劳动法》
Labor Law of the People's Republic of China

《中华人民共和国老年人权益保障法》
Law of the People's Republic of China on the Protection of the Rights and Interests of the Elderly

《中华人民共和国领海及毗连区法》
Law of the People's Republic of China on Territorial Seas and Adjacent Zones

《中华人民共和国律师法》
Lawyers Law of the People's Republic of China

《中华人民共和国煤炭法》
Coal Law of the People's Republic of China

《中华人民共和国民法通则》
General Rules (or Principles) of the Civil Law of the People's Republic of China

《中华人民共和国民事诉讼法》
Civil Procedure Law of the People's Republic of China

《中华人民共和国民用航空法》
Civil Aviation Law of the People's Republic of China

《中华人民共和国民族区域自治法》
Law of the People's Republic of China on Regional National Autonomy

《中华人民共和国母婴保健法》
Law of the People's Republic of China on Health Protection of Mothers and Infants

《中华人民共和国农业法》
Agriculture Law of the People's Republic of China

《中华人民共和国农业技术推广法》
Law of the People's Republic of China on Agro-technical Popu-

larization

《中华人民共和国拍卖法》
Auction Law of the People's Republic of China

《中华人民共和国票据法》
Law of the People's Republic of China on Negotiable Instruments

《中华人民共和国企业破产法(试行)》
Law of the People's Republic of China on Enterprise Bankruptcy (for Trial Implementation)

中华人民共和国全国人民代表大会
the National People's Congress (NPC) of the People's Republic of China

中华人民共和国全国人民代表大会常务委员会(全国人大常委会)
the Standing Committee of the National People's Congress of the People's Republic of China

《中华人民共和国全国人民代表大会和地方各级人民代表大会代表法》
Law of the People's Republic of China on Deputies to the National People's Congress and the Local People's Congresses at Various Levels

《中华人民共和国全国人民代表大会和地方各级人民代表大会选举法》
Electoral Law of the People's Republic of China for the National People's Congress and the Local People's Congresses at Various Levels

《中华人民共和国全国人民代表大会组织法》
Organic Law of the National People's Congress of the People's Republic of China

《中华人民共和国全民所有制工业企业法》
Law of the People's Republic of China on Industrial Enterprises Owned by the Whole People

《中华人民共和国人民法院组织法》
Organic Law of the People's Courts of the People's Republic of China

《中华人民共和国人民防空法》
Civil Air Defense Law of the People's Republic of China

《中华人民共和国人民检察院组织法》
Organic Law of the People's Procuratorates of the People's Republic of China

《中华人民共和国人民警察法》
Law of the People's Republic of China on the People's Police

《中华人民共和国森林法》
Forestry Law of the People's Republic of China

《中华人民共和国商标法》
Trademark Law of the People's Republic of China

《中华人民共和国商业银行法》
Law of the People's Republic of China on Commercial Banks

《中华人民共和国涉外经济合同法》
Law of the People's Republic of China on Economic Contracts Involving Foreign Interests

《中华人民共和国审计法》
Auditing Law of the People's Republic of China

《中华人民共和国食品卫生法》
Food Hygiene Law of the People's Republic of China

《中华人民共和国收养法》
Adoption Law of the People's Republic of China

《中华人民共和国水法》
Water Law of the People's Republic of China

《中华人民共和国水土保持法》
Law of the People's Republic of China on Water and Soil Conservation

《中华人民共和国水污染防治法》
Law of the People's Republic of China on the Prevention and Control of Water Pollution

《中华人民共和国税收征收管理法》
Law of the People's Republic of China on the Collection and Management of Taxes

《中华人民共和国台湾同胞投资保护法》
Law of the People's Republic of China on the Protection of Investment by Compatriots in Taiwan

《中华人民共和国体育法》
Physical Culture Law of the People's Republic of China

《中华人民共和国铁路法》
Law of the People's Republic of China on Railways

《中华人民共和国统计法》
Statistics Law of the People's Republic of China

《中华人民共和国土地管理法》
Land Administration Law of the People's Republic of China

《中华人民共和国外国人入境出境管理法》
Law of the People's Republic of China on the Control of Entry and Exit of Aliens

《中华人民共和国外商投资企业和外国企业所得税法》
Income Tax Law of the People's Republic of China for Foreign-Invested Enterprises and Foreign Businesses

《中华人民共和国外资企业法》
Law of the People's Republic of China on Foreign-Capital Enterprises

《中华人民共和国未成年人保护法》
Law of the People's Republic of China on the Protection of Juveniles

《中华人民共和国文物保护法》
Law of the People's Republic of China on the Protection of Cultural Relics

《中华人民共和国宪法》
Constitution of the People's Republic of China

《中华人民共和国献血法》
Law of the People's Republic of China on Donating Blood

《中华人民共和国乡镇企业法》
Law of the People's Republic of China on Town and Township Enterprises

《中华人民共和国香港特别行政区基本法》
Basic Law of the Hong Kong Special Administrative Region of the People's Republic of China

《中华人民共和国香港特别行政区驻军法》
Garrison Law of（the People's Liberation Army Troops Stationed in）the Hong Kong Special Administrative Region of the People's Republic of China

《中华人民共和国消防法》
Law of the People's Republic of China on Fire Prevention and Control

《中华人民共和国消费者权益保障法》
Law of the People's Republic of China on the Protection of the Rights and Interests of Consumers

《中华人民共和国刑法》
Criminal Law of the People's Republic of China

《中华人民共和国刑事诉讼法》
Criminal Procedure Law of the People's Republic of China

《中华人民共和国行政处罚法》
Administrative Penalty Law of the People's Republic of China

《中华人民共和国行政监察法》
Administrative Supervision Law of the People's Republic of China

《中华人民共和国行政诉讼法》
Administrative Procedure Law of the People's Republic of China

《中华人民共和国烟草专卖法》
Tobacco Monopoly Law of the People's Republic of China

《中华人民共和国药品管理法》
Pharmaceutical Administration Law of the People's Republic of China

《中华人民共和国野生动物保护法》
Law of the People's Republic of China on the Protection of Wild Animals

《中华人民共和国义务教育法》
Compulsory Education Law of the People's Republic of China

《中华人民共和国邮政法》
Postal Law of the People's Republic of China

《中华人民共和国渔业法》
Fisheries Law of the People's Republic of China

《中华人民共和国预备役军官法》
Law of the People's Republic of China on the Reserve Officers

《中华人民共和国预算法》
Budget Law of the People's Republic of China

《中华人民共和国证券法》
Securities Law of the People's Republic of China

《中华人民共和国中国人民银行法》
Law of the People's Republic of China on the People's Bank of China

《中华人民共和国中外合资经营企业法》
Law of the People's Republic of China on Chinese-Foreign Joint Ventures

《中华人民共和国中外合作经营企业法》
Law of the.People's Republic of China on Chinese-Foreign Co-operative Enterprises

《中华人民共和国仲裁法》
Arbitration Law of the People's Republic of China

《中华人民共和国执业医师法》
Qualified Doctors Law of the People's Republic of China

《中华人民共和国职业教育法》
Law of the People's Republic of China on Vocational Education

中华人民共和国主席
President of the People's Republic of China

《中华人民共和国注册会计师法》
Certified Accountants Law of the People's Republic of China

《中华人民共和国著作权法》
Copyright Law of the People's Republic of China

《中华人民共和国专利法》
Patent Law of the People's Republic of China

《中华人民共和国专属经济区和大陆架法》
Law of the People's Republic of China on Exclusive Economic Zones and Continental Shelves

中美三个联合公报
the three Sino-US Joint Communiques

中外合资经营企业
Chinese-foreign joint venture

中外合作经营企业
Chinese-foreign cooperative enterprise

中西部地区
the central and western parts of the country; central and western regions

中央财政收入
the central government revenue

中央军事委员会
the Military Commission of the Central Committee; the Central Military Commission

中央银行的监管作用

the supervisory role of the central bank

zhòng

重点大学
key university

重点建设项目
key construction project

重点学科、专业
key disciplines and specialties

重工业
heavy industry

重在建设
lay emphasis on progress

zhōu

周边国家
surrounding countries

周边环境
the relations with the surrounding countries; peripheral environment

zhú

逐步缩小地区发展差距
minimize (or narrow) regional development disparities step by step

zhù

住房公积金

public accumulation funds for housing

住房制度改革
reform of the housing system

著作权
copyright; right of authorship

zhuā

抓好大的(国有企业),放活小的(国有企业)
manage large (state-owned) enterprises well while adopting a flexible policy toward small ones

抓住机遇
seize (current) opportunities

"抓住机遇、深化改革、扩大开放、促进发展、保持稳定"的基本方针
the basic principle of "seizing current opportunities to deepen the reform and open China wider to the outside world, promote development and maintain stability"

zhuān

专利管理机关
patent administrative authorities

专利合作
patent cooperation

专利权
patent right; patent

专利制度
patent system

专门人才
professional personnel; specialized personnel

zhuǎn

转变政府职能
alter the functions of the government

转换企业经营机制
change (or alter) the way enterprises operate; change the way of running enterprises; change the operating mechanism of enterprises

zī

资本金制度
capital system; system of capital funds

资本市场
capital market

资本运作效率
the efficiency of the operation of capital

资本组织形式
form of capital organization

资产重组
rearrangement of assets

资产经营［评估］
operation［assessment］of assets

资源保护［更新，开发，管理］
conservation［renewal, development, management］of（natural）resources

资源节约
economical use of resources; economizing on resources

资源优化配置
optimal allocation of resources

资源有偿使用制度
a system of paid use of resources

zì

自负盈亏
assume responsibility for one's own profits or losses

自力更生
self-reliance; regeneration through one's own efforts

自强不息
constantly strive to become stronger; make unremitting efforts to improve oneself; unceasing self-improvement

自然科学
natural sciences

自然灾害的防治
the prevention and control of natural disasters

自然灾害的监测预报
the monitoring and forecasting of natural disasters

自然资源综合利用
comprehensive utilization of natural resources

自我发展
self-development

自我约束
self-restraint

自学成才
self-taught; become educated through independent study

自主创新
independent innovation (or creation)

自主经营
independent operation; operate independently

zōng

宗教活动管理
the administration of religious activities

宗教活动场所管理
the administration of sites for religious activities

宗教团体
religious organization; religious body

宗教团体和宗教事务不受外国势力的支配
China's religious bodies and religious affairs are not subject to any foreign domination

宗教信仰自由的法律保护
legal protection of the freedom of religious belief

宗教信仰自由的司法行政保障和监督
judicial and administrative guarantees and supervision of the freedom of religious belief

宗教信仰自由政策
the policy of freedom of religious belief

宗教要与社会的发展和文明的进步相适应
see that religions adapt to social development and cultural progress

宗教与教育分离的原则
the principle of separating religion from education

综合国力
overall national strength; overall strength of the country

zǒng

总设计师
chief architect

总书记
general secretary

zǒu

《走向 21 世纪的亚太经合组织科技产业合作议程》
APEC Agenda for Science and Technology Industry Cooperation into the 21st Century

走有中国特色的精兵之路
take the road of fewer but better troops with Chinese characteristics; streamline the army the Chinese way

走在时代前列
advance in the forefront of the times

zǔ

祖国统一
reunification of the motherland

zuì

最低工资保障制度
the system to ensure minimum wages; a minimum-wage guarantee system

最低生活保障制度
a system for ensuring a minimum standard of living

最高人民法院[检察院]
the Supreme People's Court [Procuratorate]

最终实现共同富裕
ultimately achieve common prosperity; the ultimate achievement of prosperity for all

zūn

尊老爱幼
respect the old and love the young

尊师重教
respect teachers and prize education; respect teachers and their teaching

尊重和保障人权
respect and guarantee human rights

尊重历史,尊重现实
respect history as well as the prevailing situation

尊重群众,尊重实践
respect the masses and value practice

尊重少数民族的风俗习惯
respect the habits and customs of the ethnic minorities

尊重知识,尊重人才
respect knowledge, respect trained personnel; respect for knowledge (or learning) and for competent people

遵纪守法
observe discipline and the law; observe discipline and abide by the law

图书在版编目(CIP)数据

汉英新时代政经用语精编/王义端,
俞颂熙编著. – 北京:外文出版社,1999.6
ISBN 7-119-02389-6

Ⅰ.汉… Ⅱ.①王… ②俞… Ⅲ.新词语-词典-汉、英
Ⅳ.Z32

中国版本图书馆 CIP 数据核字(1999)第 10019 号

外文出版社网址:
  http://www.flp.com.cn
外文出版社电子信箱:
  info@flp.com.cn
  sales@flp.com.cn

汉英新时代政经用语精编

作 者	王义端 俞颂熙
责任编辑	陈 凯
封面设计	蔡 荣
出版发行	外文出版社
社 址	北京市百万庄大街24号 邮政编码 100037
电 话	(010)68320579(总编室)
	(010)68329514 / 68327211(推广发行部)
印 刷	春雷印刷厂
经 销	新华书店 / 外文书店
开 本	34 开(119×185 毫米) 字 数 150千字
印 数	0001—3000 册 印 张 11
版 次	1999 年 6 月第 1 版第 1 次印刷
装 别	平
书 号	ISBN 7 – 119 – 02389 – 6 /H·784(外)
定 价	19.50 元